A

MEXICO

edited by ROBERT EMMET LONG

THE REFERENCE SHELF

Volume 58 Number 4

THE H. W. WILSON COMPANY

New York   1986

THE REFERENCE SHELF

The books in this series contain reprints of articles, excerpts from books, and addresses on current issues and social trends in the United States and other countries. There are six separately bound numbers in each volume, all of which are generally published in the same calendar year. One number is a collection of recent speeches; each of the others is devoted to a single subject and gives background information and discussion from various points of view, concluding with a comprehensive bibliography. Books in the series may be purchased individually or on subscription.

Library of Congress Cataloging in Publication Data

Main entry under title:

Mexico.

(The Reference shelf ; v. 58, no. 4)
Bibliography: p.
1. Mexico—Economic conditions—1970–
2. Rural–urban migration—Mexico.   3. Mexico—Emigration and immigration.   I. Long, Robert Emmet.   II. Series.
HC135.M254   1986   330.972'0834   86–15892
ISBN 0–8242–0726–2

Printed in the United States of America

CONTENTS

III. Problems at Mexico's Borders

PREFACE

In the early 1970s, due largely to the development of its vast petroleum reserves, Mexico seemed to be entering an era of unprecedented prosperity. In this time of euphoric expectations, corporate investment expanded enormously, and Mexico's oil industry soon became the fourth largest in the world. At the same time Mexico became a force in the political life of Central America, opposing U.S. intervention in the region, maintaining cordial relations with the Soviet-Cuban block, and acting generally as the Caribbean Basin's "Big Brother." Beginning in 1982, however, as José Lopez Portillo left office and Miguel de la Madrid assumed the presidency, Mexico's economy unraveled. The instigating factor in this collapse was a worldwide overproduction of oil and subsequent decline in oil prices. Since over seventy percent of Mexico's industrial earnings derive from its oil industry, the drop in oil prices was particularly devastating. Mexico's enormous foreign debt, assumed to underwrite a decade of industrial expansion, could no longer be met. Although its loan payments to U.S. and other banks have been extended, Mexico can hardly repay even the interest on the loans, much less the principal, which now amounts to $100 billion. From soaring expectations, Mexico has been plunged into a state of severe and apparently unresolvable crisis.

This compilation examines the state of Mexico today. The opening and largest section addresses the current economic crisis, its background, as well as its implications for many aspects of Mexican life. Domestic and foreign politics have both been affected by Mexico's enormous foreign debt, and accompanying austerity, bringing a diminished ability to influence affairs in Central America. Also examined, as one of the many problems slowing and perhaps preventing economic recovery, is the issue of corruption in the Mexican political-economic system, a factor in the mismanagement of the country's economy. A second section focuses upon another troubling aspect of Mexican life—the migration from rural areas to Mexico City, which has grown so rapidly that urban planners have barely been able to cope with the city's chronic poverty and pollution, its shortages of water and sewage disposal facilities. The dilemmas of Mexico City, as later articles in this section illustrate, have been made particularly dramatic by the devastating earthquake that occurred in 1985. The final section treats another aspect of the crisis in Mexico—how it causes as well as affects the handling of problems at Mexico's borders. From the south comes an influx of Guatemalan refugees, whereas in the north a flood of Mexicans seeks economic relief in the U.S. All these sections bear ultimately on Mexico's depressed economy, a situation offering little hope for improvement in the foreseeable future.

The editor is indebted to the authors and publishers who have granted permission to reprint materials in this compilation. Special thanks are due to Ellen Morin and the Fulton Public Library, and to the staff of the Penfield Library, State University of New York at Oswego.

Robert Emmet Long

June 1986

I. MEXICO'S CRISIS

EDITOR'S INTRODUCTION

Since Miguel de la Madrid came to the presidency in 1982, efforts have been made to deal with Mexico's economic crisis. A program of austerity has compelled business and industry to live within their means, and legislation has been introduced to curb corruption in business and government. But these measures, although a responsible and a steadying influence on the country, have not provided long-term solutions. Mexico's foreign debt, indeed, has actually increased from $80 to $100 billion, and unemployment is now higher than before. Commentators on Mexico have been concerned with these trends, as well as with the damage that the economy has suffered.

This section examines Mexico's economic crisis and points out some of the social and political problems that are preventing the recovery of the economy from its present stagnation. The many issues involved are outlined by President de la Madrid in excerpts from an article reprinted from *Foreign Affairs*. Defending his administration, President de la Madrid stresses advances made in internal and external affairs. Jorge G. Castañeda, also writing in *Foreign Affairs*, puts the President's remarks in perspective in an informed review of Mexico's political system. In particular he emphasizes the Revolutionary Institutional Party (PRI), which has been in power uninterruptedly for fifty years. In light of this system, Castañeda doubts whether de la Madrid has the mandate to undertake the sizable reforms now needed. Forrest D. Colburn, writing for *The New Leader*, highlights one issue in particular, blaming government ownership of much of Mexico's business for the waste and inefficiency that continues to assault the already shaky economy and limit the effectiveness of a strict austerity program. The fourth article, by John S. De Mott, a *Time* staffwriter, recounts Mexico's struggle to live up to its financial commitments and the effect austerity has had on the economy.

Economic chaos has created and/or magnified other problems in Mexican society that are analyzed in three articles from *Current History*. First Bruce Michael Bagley deals with the impact of a crippled economy on Mexico's foreign policy. He is particularly pessimistic about the effectiveness of Mexico as a leader among developing nations and in Central America while it carries $100 billion in foreign debt. The state of the oil industry, another area of crucial concern, is described by George W. Grayson as a reflection of its unique status as a government monopoly. Though it is badly in need of reform, it is also the main source of badly needed foreign exchange and therefore must not be destabilized. The effects of the financial crisis caused by falling oil prices on Mexican plans for increasing the national standard of living are described by James H. Street. Afflicted with the waste and inefficiency already touched on in this section, PEMEX (Petroleos Mexicanos) has been practically destroyed by corruption. 'La Mordida' (the bite) must be stopped and yet it is so deeply rooted no one dares to touch it. Excerpts from an article by Flavio Tavares, reprinted from *World Press Review*, enlarged upon the scandals involving Pemex executives as well as its union leaders, who are influential in the PRI. If such a system is examined too closely everyone, including President de la Madrid, will be vulnerable. Rod Norland, a *Newsweek* staffwriter, concludes with a description of this problem that shows it to be so epidemic that it seems to preclude any possibility of economic health.

MEXICO: THE NEW CHALLENGES[1]

In 1985, Mexico will commemorate the seventy-fifth anniversary of its revolution. A new political system and social order was founded after 1910, which modernized our nation within a climate of democratic freedom and political stability. Now, toward the end of the century, Mexico faces harsh new challenges. Our economic

[1]Excerpts from an article by Miguel de la Madrid H., President of Mexico. Reprinted by permission from *Foreign Affairs*, 63:62–76. Fall '84. Copyright © 1984 by *Foreign Affairs*.

development has brought structural imbalances which must be corrected, and we face the immediate impacts of external pressures, the international economic situation, and conflicts afflicting the international system in Central America, the Middle East and other regions of the world.

Contrary to predictions made two years ago, at the height of our crisis, when some said Mexico's capacity to maintain political stability and an adequate functioning economy was in doubt, the progress attained in overcoming our most critical difficulties is widely recognized today.

My government and the Mexican people have confronted severe tests of endurance. We have had to respond with drastic economic adjustment measures to resume a sustained recovery. We instituted reforms to strengthen the honesty and efficiency of the government. We are conducting a responsible foreign policy and, most important, we have drawn strength from the exemplary solidarity of our different social groups. Our citizens' participation has been decisive in overcoming the crisis.

Mexico is reaffirming its fundamental values. To the extent that we are able to maintain our nationalism, the commitment to satisfy the basic needs of our population, and our respect for law and democratic freedoms, our society will remain united. The greatest challenge we face at present is to translate these essential principles into new forms of public and social action.

Our country's achievements and basic strengths can be understood only through an appreciation of the way our major social movements and unique political institutions developed over time.

After three centuries of colonial domination, Mexico was a predominantly agrarian and mineral-exporting country which had provided the largest single source of income for the Spanish Crown. The first struggle to inspire a broad-based movement of the Mexican people was the War of Independence that started in 1810. The national government was recognized in 1824, but the task of creating a sovereign and united nation persisted.

The governments that followed had to confront semi-autonomous regional centers of power, a traditional church and army, linguistic and cultural differences, and the extreme poverty of more than 90 percent of the population. Internal difficulties and external intervention led to the loss of half of Mexico's territory to the United States in 1847. Over the next two decades, liberal and democratic reforms were taken to overcome the remnants of the colonial order and guarantee the sovereignty of the new nation-state, unifying the Mexican people to victory over the French expeditionary force and its conservative supporters in 1867.

Toward the end of the nineteenth century, the economic infrastructure for development began to take shape. The three decades of General Porfirio Díaz's dictatorship (1876–1910), however, brought extreme concentration of wealth, land and political power, eroding the legitimacy and viability of the regime and its capacity to promote further internal growth. The regime was unable to transfer political power peacefully to a new government. This, combined with adverse internal and international economic conditions, led to social unrest and increased demands for political democracy. It accentuated national outrage over the foreign control of our national resources.

Mexico's revolution started in 1910. It sought to recover the ideals of the nineteenth-century liberal-democratic movement and to carry out land reform, labor rights, and national control of our resources. Over one million lives were lost. Only the establishment of a new social covenant, the 1917 Constitution, ended the violence.

This Constitution governs Mexico today. It is based on nationalism, the nation's will to become a vigorous and independent community. Mexican nationalism implies a deep awareness of our cultural identity, enriched by our own diversity, and the commitment to defend our country from any threat to its independence. In contrast to European nationalism, which was essentially conservative, ours mobilizes the social forces of the country in a common purpose of protecting our democracy—not only in strictly political terms but also as a way of carrying out significant improvements in the social and cultural conditions of our population.

The revolutionary leadership after 1917 set out to resume economic development, and institutionalized the political framework by unifying contending forces in the revolution's political party in 1929. In the 1930s, Mexico achieved peaceful and orderly trans-

fers of power. We also recovered sovereignty over our oil resources, carried out an extensive land reform and furthered the
goals of free public education and progressive labor relations.
Since then, the labor movement, peasant organizations, the middle
class and the private sector have had effective institutional channels to promote their interests; their orderly participation has
helped to consolidate the political regime.

The basic institutions and rules of the political system were
established with the founding of the party of the revolution, now
the Revolutionary Institutional Party (PRI), and have been
strengthened since: a strong one-term presidency; guarantee of
democratic freedoms for all citizens; respect and loyalty of the
armed forces for the Constitution and the political system; mechanisms for reaching policy agreements by negotiation; and a permanent process of strengthening social rights through legal reforms
and increasing the social benefits to public education, health and
municipal services. . . .

During these last few years, not only Mexico's political institutions, but its social fabric as well, have had to face new challenges. The urgent task has been to meet the basic needs of a
population which has grown from 20 to 76 million in scarcely four
decades. Mexico is now the eleventh largest nation in the world.
Once an agrarian society, we now have two-thirds of our population living in urban areas. Rapid economic growth and urbanization have generated additional demands and created new
problems.

Mexico stands as one of the world's most successful cases of
economic growth. Over four decades it maintained an annual
growth rate of more than six percent. Its productive capacity is
now the ninth largest in the world, excluding the East European
socialist countries. Its natural resources are diverse and abundant;
its hydrocarbon reserves are the fourth largest in the world, and
it is one of the main producers of metallic and non-metallic miner-
als. Its agriculture is diversified and its industry bigger than that
of some developed countries, such as Sweden, Belgium, Denmark,
Norway and Spain, and developing countries such as South Korea
and India. We have built an extensive and modern transport in-

frastructure, and our tourist and commercial services can compete with the best in the world. The quality of our human resources has also been significantly improved through the creation of important research centers and extensive higher education and technical facilities. Overall, the gains made in production, employment and basic services are significant.

Improvements in health care made us one of the fastest growing populations in the world. The population of Mexico City and the metropolitan zone is equal to that of all Central America. A way had to be found to reduce this growth without infringing upon individual rights. The solution was to promote family planning, which allowed us to reduce the annual rate of growth from an average of 3.2 percent during the decade 1970–80 to 2.4 percent in 1984.

Despite the population increase in the last decade, the number of people having access to higher education and training facilities tripled and over 70 percent of all housing now has water and electricity. Illiteracy has dropped from 26 percent of the population to 17 percent. Every child is now guaranteed access to elementary school. Education is clearly the key to the major changes that have taken place in Mexico over the past 50 years.

Yet, extreme social inequalities persist and the country has had to overcome an acute economic crisis. Our economy was not structured to withstand external shocks. The heavy reliance on internal industrial growth had not been accompanied by commercial modernization and increases in agricultural productivity. Internal financing was insufficient to meet the demographic pressures as they were translated into growing social demands for public expenditure and investment. An overvalued exchange rate inhibited industrial integration and competitiveness and made capital exports and foreign purchases very profitable. High oil prices and corresponding credit availability allowed us to survive such imbalances, but when the price of oil fell, expectations were modified, our disequilibriums became apparent and a chain of reactions occurred which deepened the crisis.

During 1982 the gross domestic product fell for the first time since the Great Crash of 1929. Inflation, which was 30 percent during the first months of 1982, soared to 150 percent by year-end. The peso was devalued 600 percent, the public sector's deficit reached almost 18 percent of the gross domestic product (GDP), and the foreign debt stood at $77 billion. . . .

Our people have understood that there was no choice but austerity. They supported the government's economic reordering program. Through concerted efforts, economic activity has been renewed. Despite the sacrifices imposed by the crisis, an open and frank dialogue has been maintained between the government and the society. The clearest proof of this is that we have been able to face our difficulties, and solve our differences without social unrest. With the strength of this domestic consensus, the economic program was implanted immediately, thus reducing the time of the adjustment and correcting the most serious structural imbalances.

Despite a five-percent fall in the GDP in 1983, the programs for maintaining basic social services, protecting jobs and the nation's productive plant helped avoid a greater deterioration of the situation. Our manufacturing industries have already shown positive signs of recovery. These measures—combined with a good agricultural year in which output increased four percent, with the emergency employment programs which generated 400,000 jobs in 1983, and with the additional absorption capacity of the informal sectors of the economy—avoided increases in the levels of unemployment.

The stabilization policy permitted a reduction of the public sector's deficit as a percentage of GDP from 18 to 8.7 percent in 1983. This was accomplished by clearly defining priorities while maintaining basic social expenditures and labor-intensive programs, reducing waste and eliminating subsidies, increasing revenue and ensuring the efficient and honest execution of the government's programs. Previous investment projects are being reevaluated according to present costs and priorities. We are limiting the growth of public spending and increasing its efficiency.

The stabilization of the economy is being accomplished without a drastic fall in productive capacity. A hyperinflationary process was avoided by reducing the rate of inflation, which in the period December 1981–December 1982 reached 99 percent, to a yearly average of 80 percent by 1983. At the same time, in our foreign sector the balance of payments achieved an unprecedented surplus, allowing us to replenish the central bank's international reserves. Our international debt obligations were met. Along with all this, we were able to restore essential imports and are starting to increase our non-oil exports.

The efforts we have made to adjust our internal imbalances have prepared us to face worldwide uncertainty and the insecurity of the mid-1980s from a stronger position than many other nations with similar problems.

These achievements are certainly promising, but there has been a fall in our population's standard of living as a result of the crisis. We are deeply concerned with the additional social costs imposed by the rise in U.S. interest rates and by trade restrictions. These reduce foreign exchange, limit the resources available for development and make recovery all the more difficult. In no way has Mexico become complacent. . . .

The international economic situation strongly influences the problems of Mexico and Latin America. Our countries are suffering from an unprecedented financial and economic crisis. The rise in interest rates, the contraction of international trade and the protectionist measures adopted by industrialized nations constitute obstacles to our recovery. These factors also aggravate the social inequalities in the region and threaten the political stability of several Latin American nations.

In the face of such conditions, it is increasingly recognized that unilateral decisions in developed countries, which fail to take into account the real possibilities for placing the economies of developing nations on a sound footing, are counterproductive. The costs are too high to be carried by one side alone. Further delays in Latin America's and Europe's recoveries would bring about global economic stagnation.

It is Mexico's conviction, more and more generalized throughout the world, that in order to overcome the international crisis, the present framework of international economic relations must be modified toward a more cooperative structure in which national economic policies will be in tune with a global need to expand trade and reduce interest rates.

For Mexico and the other Latin American countries, the rise of interest rates severely restricts spending on essential social programs, reduces new investments in the private sector, drastically increases the cost of internal credit and upsets the balance of payments. This situation, together with the international trade restrictions, has exerted extreme pressure on our ability to repay foreign debts and threatens to perpetuate the situation by making financing of economic development practically inaccessible.

Now more than ever, increased exports from developing countries mean not only added capacity to import goods and to service the foreign debt, but also higher levels of economic activity and employment in developed nations. Simultaneously, net flows of resources to developing nations must be reestablished in order to secure the partial economic recovery begun in 1983.

Unilateral increases in interest rates nullify a large part of the difficult adjustment process that has been implemented at a high social cost in many Latin American nations. For this reason, there is a growing consensus on the need for debtors to participate on an equal basis with creditors in the process of reordering the international economy and promoting the new operative mechanisms necessary to permit debtor countries to restructure their debts under conditions that allow a lasting recovery.

The current crisis should alert the international community to the need for joint action based on regional cooperation and respect for the interests of both debtors and creditors. Efforts should be directed toward strengthening the international economic recovery as well as the capacity of individual countries to meet their obligations. Otherwise, the accumulation of unilateral increases in interest rates could lead to unilateral reactions which would abruptly cut off any possibility for less costly solutions for either the nations involved or the international economy as a whole.

For Mexico, the affairs of war or peace in Central America and the course of our economic and financial relations with the United States are necessarily defined by the perspective of our relationship with Latin America. Because of historical identity, cultural unity and common economic interests, our destiny is intimately linked to that of all Latin American countries.

Worsening economic pressures on the debt and international trade, together with the political tensions existing in Central America, have strengthened, more than ever, our conviction that only by fully cooperating with other Latin American nations, Canada and the United States can a better future be built for Mexico and the continent.

We are realistically facing the necessary internal reordering of our economies. What is required is that industrialized nations carry out coherent economic policies that avoid the transfer of the costs of recovery to developing nations, and which set the basis for a more equal world economic order. . . .

MEXICO AT THE BRINK[2]

Mexico's famed political stability has not been destroyed by the country's current economic crisis. But that stability can no longer be taken for granted.

Over the past half-century, the Mexican political system has brought economic development, albeit unjustly distributed, inefficiently planned and plagued with waste and corruption. It has ensured social peace and political continuity, although with recurrent repression and electoral fraud. And it has maintained peaceful relations with the United States, despite asymmetries, irritants and sporadic confrontations. These three pillars of Mexico's stability, which is unique in Latin America, are not yet crumbling, but all are growing weaker, as is the political system they sustain.

The causes of Mexico's deepest crisis in modern times are clearly economic; the crisis is rooted in the country's 1982 financial crash and has been compounded since then by economic stagnation, austerity measures and the devastating earthquakes that

[2]Reprint of an article by Jorge G. Castañeda, Professor of Political Science at the National University of Mexico, and Senior Associate at the Carnegie Endowment for International Peace in Washington, D.C. Reprinted by permission from *Foreign Affairs*, 64:287-303. Winter '85/'86. Copyright © 1985 by *Foreign Affairs*.

hit Mexico in September. But the most immediate and acute expression of the crisis is political. Though the consequences of a breakdown in the political system would be chiefly domestic, there could be grave repercussions for the United States.

President Miguel de la Madrid has encountered many unsolvable problems since he took office in December 1982: a present-day $100-billion foreign debt; a five percent drop in GNP in 1983 with no prospect of renewed economic growth; rampant corruption at most levels of national life; a country disappointed in itself, questioning its direction. But the principal challenge the president, and Mexico, face today is the total lack of credibility in the political system.

Results from a poll taken last June and published in *Excelsior*, Mexico's leading daily, underline this fact. When asked whether government officials lied or told the truth in stating that the country was emerging from its economic crisis, 88 percent of those interviewed replied that the officials were lying. Likewise, when asked if they believed whether the results of the then upcoming elections would be respected, 55 percent said no, and only 13 percent answered in the affirmative.

II

The country's long-lasting stability comes from a combination of just enough democracy: elections, at least in name; a certain freedom of the press; a degree of tolerance for most forms of opposition; and just enough authoritarianism: electoral fraud; silencing excessive criticism of the government and the president; cooptation, corruption and repression, in that order, of the insufficiently loyal opposition. The Revolutionary Institutional Party (PRI) has been in power for five decades, but no president has succeeded himself. The only one elected to a second term, Alvaro Obregon in 1928, was assassinated. Thus, while the faces and the ways of climbing the political ladder may change (if not the ideas), the so-called political class has maintained its hold on power.

Through the years, the system's mainstays—the organized labor movement, the peasantry and the federal and local bureaucracies—were kept happy, loyal and politically apathetic by the trickling down of just enough economic growth, job creation, land distribution and social services. Even the new urban middle classes created by this economic growth, which averaged six percent a year from 1940 to 1982, were incorporated into the system. Thanks to a high degree of social mobility and cheap, readily available dollars before 1982, they were assured relatively easy access to a modern, affluent way of life.

The country's lack of democracy was not perceived to be a problem. True, the PRI had won every presidential, gubernatorial and senatorial election, and 95 percent of all congressional and municipal seats, since 1934. But being unaccustomed to free elections, public debate, a critical press or an accountable government, Mexico's Babbitts were content with continual improvements in their living standards. Little did they mind the backwardness of a political system increasingly at odds with a rapidly modernizing society.

Thanks to its traditional vote-gathering mechanisms in the countryside, in the poorer southern states, and within certain sectors of the labor movement and federal bureaucracy, the party has won, and generally will continue to win, with no more than its usual doses of electoral fraud. Mexico has long been accustomed to evident but limited amounts of fraud in many places, or to extensive yet discreet ballot-stuffing and polling booth intimidation in a few localized areas. On the whole, voters have accepted a generous amount of this electoral "alchemy," as it is known in Mexico, as a fact of their political life.

The 1968 student movement, quashed by the massacre of more than 400 demonstrators, was an early but largely unheeded warning that Mexican society was changing. Subsequent governments reacted by providing a little more democracy and, for a while, much more economic growth. It should have been the other way around. When, by 1982, in spite of massive oil finds and a superb international credit rating, high levels of economic growth could no longer be sustained, the mistaken ways of previous years caught up with the system.

Mexico's overriding political problem stems from a simple and unalterable fact: the system, which has been traditionally clumsy in its handling of the middle classes, can no longer deliver the economic growth and prosperity that these classes now expect as a matter of course. At the same time, the political system does not feel it can grant them the additional measure of democracy which might be an acceptable alternative. Political wisdom dictates that one does not open up a political system in the midst of a severe economic crisis. Not, in any case, if one wishes to remain in power.

Surprisingly, President De la Madrid did toy with the idea of political liberalization in 1983, the first year of the drastic economic adjustment. The outcome of municipal elections in the northern border state of Chihuahua, one of the most modern and wealthy, was fully respected. The decision proved a disaster for the ruling party; the conservative, middle-class, pro-U.S. Party of National Action (PAN) swept the seven main city councils, and won the mayoral races in both Chihuahua, the state capital, and Ciudad Juárez, the country's fourth largest city.

The timid experiment in democracy was nipped in the bud. The following year, the PRI handily won municipal races in Mexicali and Tijuana, large and prosperous border communities; in several cities of Sinaloa, an affluent agricultural state on the Pacific coast; and in the central city of Puebla. Similarly, PRI victories were announced in local elections in the communities of Piedras Negras, Frontera and Monclova in the border state of Coahuila at the end of 1984. But the opposition protested what it saw as massive electoral fraud by the authorities; the protests, as well as local internal divisions within the PRI, led to widespread violence in Piedras Negras and Monclova. Concerned by the implications of riots and civil strife along the U.S. border, President De la Madrid ordered the army into Piedras Negras. The violence was quickly halted, but the solution was possibly more provocative than the problem itself.

The PAN, most of the participating leftist groups and many independent observers felt that, had the election results been respected as in Chihuahua, the PAN would have won most of these races. There are a number of reasons for this assessment. Mexico's northern region has borne the brunt of the economic crisis, particularly the states of Baja California, Sonora, Chihuahua, Coahuila and Nuevo León. The frequent devaluations of the Mexican peso (from 25 pesos to the dollar in February 1982 to almost 500 pesos as of November 1985) have had a devastating effect on this region, whose economy has more extensive links to the United States than the rest of the country.

In addition, the region's close contact with the United States leads its inhabitants to compare their living standards and political fate with those of their U.S. neighbors. Such comparisons are delicate, though inevitable; they tend to fuel unrealistic and unfulfillable expectations. Also, since the north is the most affluent part of the country, along with parts of Mexico City, its population is more demanding and critical of the government's typical corruption, cronyism, waste and general incompetence.

Disaffection in urban areas was evident in national congressional elections held last July 7. Although the official returns showed that the PRI obtained 65 percent of the vote nationally, it polled less than 45 percent in the nation's five largest cities combined: the capital, Guadalajara, Ciudad Nezahualcoyotl (outside Mexico City), Monterrey and Juárez. The PAN's share of the vote, again according to the official count, was reported to be 15.6 percent nationwide.

It is difficult to ascertain what the real results of these elections would have been if there had been no fraud. Independent analysts and most opposition parties on both the right and the left have estimated that the nationwide fraud in favor of the PRI hovered around nine percent. If so, the PRI's true score would not be 65 percent but approximately 56 percent, and that of the PAN about 22–23 percent.

Reliable estimates of fraud at the local level are next to impossible to make. According to most accounts, it was so widespread in the northern states of Nuevo León and Sonora that the official election results for those states were meaningless. In seven of the country's eight most populous and prosperous states (the Federal District, Jalisco, the state of Mexico, Chihuahua, Nuevo León, Baja California and Sonora), which make up 42 percent of the registered voting population, the PRI won less than 55 percent of the vote. This estimate is based on official figures for five of the states and conservative estimates for Sonora and Nuevo León, where the PAN's support is strongest. An estimate of the PAN's true score over all seven states would be about 25 percent.

The magnitude of fraud does not mean that the PRI would have necessarily lost if free and fair elections had been held. The point is that the opposition, though still a minority, is larger in some areas than the national tally indicates, even when adjusted for fraud. More important, these estimates indicate that the PRI is losing its electoral hold in the urban, middle-income, "modernized" classes in the north and to a lesser extent in the central region.

The political system as a whole has already lost the support of the prosperous, "developed" segments of Mexican society. It is no longer truly representative of key social strata such as lawyers, doctors, accountants, lower-income clerks, shop owners and even some local bureaucrats and industrial workers. They may be equally disenchanted with the existing opposition, but they no longer believe in the government or look to Mexico City for the solution of their region's problems. In fact, many Mexican observers see increasing signs of a slow awakening in certain northern communities of a dormant streak in Mexican consciousness favoring closer links with the United States.

Losing the votes of these key sectors does not necessarily mean that the PRI will lose power on a national level through electoral defeat, but it does represent a serious weakening of the PRI's long-standing dominance. This trend calls into question the viability of a one-party monopoly of political power. There is a growing cleavage separating the modern, northern, urban, more affluent Mexico, where the PRI barely receives a plurality or a slight majority of the vote, and the backward, southern, rural and poorer Mexico, where it continues to rack up 80–90 percent of the vote. The PRI rules both Mexicos as if they were one; they are not. Such a situation eventually seems untenable without coercion. And somewhere along the line coercion implies the military; everyone knows how its involvement begins, but no one ever knows how it ends.

In those cases where more than "traditional" fraud is needed to secure a PRI victory, or where voters no longer accept even the usual amount of fraud, the government will increasingly run up against the choice it faced in Piedras Negras: either give in to the opposition, or call in the army. This is a no-win choice.

III

Since the 1930s, the Mexican armed forces have rarely meddled in politics; they have respected civilian rule and have seldom been called upon to repair the system's malfunctions. Although the army was called on to deal with minor electoral problems during the early 1960s, the last time it intervened because of a serious breakdown was in 1968, when negotiations between the government and the student movement collapsed two weeks before the inauguration of the Olympic Games. In the mid-1970s, the army suppressed a guerrilla uprising in the state of Guerrero, but this incursion into political matters was limited to an isolated region.

There is certainly no immediate risk of greater army involvement in political matters, but there could be in the future. Indeed, the military seems to be suffering less from the system's general discredit than other sectors. According to a poll taken in mid-1985, when Mexicans were asked to state which elements of society "lie" more to the public, 59 percent gave politicians as their first answer, 26 percent mentioned public officials first, but only two percent of those interviewed considered the military to be more untruthful than other elements. True, the September earthquakes may have damaged the army's image somewhat, but more because of what it did not do. Troops were called out to patrol the city and prevent looting, but they did not actively participate in relief and rescue operations.

More important, however, there are reasons for believing that, for the first time in years, a serious split has developed within the army and between the military and the government. According to certain sources, many middle-level, relatively young (ages 35 to 45) and well-educated officers are particularly upset about the passive role the government and the higher military echelons obliged the armed forces to play in the immediate aftermath of the quakes. This split could be the most important political trend to emerge from September's tragedy.

The potential for unrest is much more widespread now than in the 1960s or 1970s. Major incidents were avoided during this year's elections in potentially explosive states such as Sonora and Nuevo León. Although unrest has not yet reached alarming levels, it easily could. The army's traditional neutrality could be eroded if the government orders it in with growing frequency to stifle protest and violence arising from true or perceived instances of electoral fraud. Sooner or later, the army would probably insist on intervening before the violence occurs, to preempt it. The army could even feel compelled to intervene before the voting itself if elections habitually result in violence. The cycle of fraud, violence and army intervention was avoided in 1985, but the pressures are there which could trigger this cycle in the gubernatorial elections in the state of Chihuahua in July 1986.

There is no realistic short-term solution to the political crisis. Opening up the political system and giving the northern middle classes an equivalent of democratic "self-rule," instead of the economic growth they previously enjoyed or the major reforms the country needs but cannot have overnight, is a desirable but not entirely viable alternative. Centrifugal forces in the north, traditional Mexican fears of U.S.-inspired division of the country, and the real and perceived risk of losing control over an unprecedented process of political liberalization make this option a nonstarter. It would take a daring, imaginative government to forestall long-term collapse at the risk of short-term political fallout; the Mexican political system does not seem up to the challenge today.

There are, however, some hopeful signs of change from the bottom up. The outpouring of solidarity, civic responsibility and participation by Mexican society that followed the September earthquakes could contribute to an initial democratization of Mexico's political institutions. For the moment, this hypothesis remains highly speculative, though it has been advanced by some of Mexico's most perceptive analysts, particularly by Carlos Monsivais, the outstanding chronicler of Mexico City's devastation. In the aftermath of the quake, some forms of grassroots organization and left-wing sponsored mobilization have emerged among the most severely affected by the tremors, such as the homeless and relatives of the dead. These embryonic signs of political consciousness could eventually evolve into new, left-leaning political organizations that would be truly independent of the government.

While Mexicans and foreigners score debating points by criticizing the weaknesses of a political system apparently incapable of living with a strong opposition, this criticism is, in a sense, less important given the current economic situation. Concessions are easier when cushioned by prosperity; the country's rulers will not loosen their grip on power unless they can make the process relatively painless through economic growth. Yet, if such growth were possible, the need for political change would not be so acute.

The scattered and relative democratic advances which the Mexican political system has known over the past 50 years have come about under extreme pressure (the Great Depression, the 1968 student movement) or in the midst of spectacular economic growth (the 1978–1981 oil boom). Under the present and vastly different conditions, such pressure could be explosively dangerous because the political system is much weaker now, and such growth is nowhere in sight. There are consequently few signs of gradual political change; nor is a scenario foreseeable for a significant political transformation.

IV

Liberalization of the political system can only come about if the country's economic difficulties are first addressed in an adequate, lasting manner. Despite a slight and short-lived recovery in late 1984 and early 1985, the Mexican economy has remained stagnant since 1982, when it suffered zero growth for the first time in years. In 1983 the economy worsened: GNP declined by 5.3 percent, and per capita income dropped nearly eight percent. 1984 brought 3.5 percent growth, but at a high cost: a new recession in 1985, with the economy barely growing one percent over the entire year. Although the cost of reconstruction after the earthquakes has not yet been determined, simply rebuilding housing for the homeless, repairing Mexico City's severely damaged drinking-water system and replacing destroyed telecommunications and medical facilities will run into the billions of dollars.

The economic adjustment program implemented by President De la Madrid—in accord with the International Monetary Fund—has allowed the country to pay the interest on its foreign debt, but at the cost of foregoing economic growth indefinitely. Unfortunately, the price of this trade-off may soon become too high, even for Mexico.

The country has made enormous efforts, and achieved some spectacular results, in its endeavor to put its financial house in order. Deficit spending as a percentage of GNP shrank from 18 percent in 1982 to six percent in 1984. The economy's traditional trade deficit was inverted: in 1983 Mexico enjoyed its first trade surplus in memory, totaling nearly $14 billion. This was repeated in 1984. Inflation, the government's and the IMF's chief concern, dropped from a runaway level of 100 percent in 1982 to a more manageable 80 percent in 1983 and 59 percent in 1984. Thanks to the system's long-standing control of the labor movement, this was achieved, remarkably, without major social unrest; there were few strikes and no urban riots or land seizures in the countryside.

But President De la Madrid has run out of time to cure the Mexican economy. Even without the earthquake, inflation in 1985 would have been roughly equivalent to that in 1984; because of the earthquake, it will probably be higher. Orthodox adjustment policies necessarily have their limits, and more daring measures have not been implemented. The severe austerity program has slashed most people's standard of living. Real wages have fallen nearly 50 percent in three years. Imports, mainly intermediate and capital goods, on which the economy depends for growth, are down from 1981 levels by nearly 65 percent. Although the government and the business sector have avoided massive layoffs, the 800,000 new jobs needed each year just to keep up with the growth in the labor force are not being created.

The economy's chief bottleneck remains the foreign debt. At $85 billion when President De la Madrid took office and $100 billion today, its service, despite some improvements in the terms of repayment, has become an intolerable burden for Mexico.

True, the international financial community has accepted multiyear reschedulings, enabling Mexico to reprogram principal payments of half its debt for 14 years. But these widely heralded agreements affect only capital; interest payments are left untouched. Latin American finance officials and bankers have known for some time that very few nations are likely to pay back all that they owe. The region's debt problem actually concerns interest payments—which may or may not continue to be honored.

In this respect, Mexico has been helped by the recent drop in interest rates: every one-point decline in the prime rate saves the country approximately $800 million a year. But real interest rates are still at unprecedented levels, and the service of Mexico's debt totaled nearly $14 billion in 1984, with a similar sum being disbursed in 1985. This amounts to between 55 and 60 percent of Mexican exports; there is simply not enough cash left over for the imports needed to renew sustained economic growth.

Nor will Mexico obtain sufficient funds on the international credit markets, and what it can obtain will simply compound its debt service dilemma. Indeed, even the new U.S. world debt strategy outlined by Secretary of the Treasury James Baker in October, calling for greater lending by commercial banks and the World Bank, does not address the key issue: the service on Mexico's debt eats up too much of the country's hard currency earnings. New lending, were it possible, simply postpones the problem, but does not solve it. Nor does it solve another bottom-line issue: capital flight. With well over $50 billion being held by Mexicans in American financial instruments, it seems clear that any long-term solution to Mexico's woes must address this matter. No country can sustain a constant drain on its assets like the one Mexico has faced in recent years.

Recent drops in the price of oil, which accounts for 75 percent of Mexico's foreign revenues, are making a bad situation worse. A collapse in petroleum prices—a distinct possibility—would undoubtedly induce national bankruptcy. And the other possible way to compensate for the country's traditionally low domestic savings rate, investment from abroad, involves a series of wrenching decisions. Although President De la Madrid has identified the choices, he has not yet made them. A number of economic liberalization and modernization measures were announced in mid-1985, but they are only small steps in this direction.

Whether for businessmen or progressive economic planners, the Mexican economy has been turned into a nightmare by 40 years of protectionism, inefficiency, massive subsidization of both consumer staples and industrial inputs, and technological backwardness. It is hamstrung by excessive red tape involving everything from foreign investment to import permits, and from export taxes to land tenure. There is wide agreement in Mexico today on the problems, and on the economic necessity of addressing them. But there is a glaring lack of consensus on when, how, and in what order reforms should be implemented.

V

The most fundamental obstacles to reform are political. The government clearly does not have the broad-based political support to carry out the structural changes which, in the short term, would entail hardship and privation for many sectors of Mexican society. In addition, President De la Madrid's left flank is not sufficiently well covered for him to carry out changes widely viewed as conservative and pro-American without incurring serious political damage.

The government, most of the business sector, many foreign bankers and investors, and a number of independent Mexican analysts have concluded that the only way to modernize the economy is through major reforms, which go against the grain of the country's recent history and economic policy. Thus, significant cuts in subsidies to consumers (chiefly public transportation and basic food staples) and to industry (chiefly inputs such as energy, imported raw materials, land and water) have become unavoidable as the money to continue financing them is no longer available.

A major cutback in the state-owned sector of the economy also appears economically necessary. Over the years, it has become a disguised and highly expensive welfare and unemployment insurance system, cushioning the impact of economic realities through takeovers of firms in financial trouble, featherbedding in healthy or strategic public-sector companies, and bureaucratic inertia. If these practices were openly recognized as a welfare system, they might be sustainable. Since they are not generally recognized as such, there is no rationale to sustain them in the face of their present economic unfeasibility.

The same argument applies to Mexico's 40-year tradition of protectionism. A complicated system of advance import permits, red tape, and tariff and non-tariff barriers have kept Mexican industry well insulated from foreign competition. Without a doubt, this contributed greatly to import substitution and the development of Mexico's modern industrial plant. But it also created a national industry which generally produces poor-quality and high-priced goods, which is totally unprepared for export-oriented growth, and which has developed a yawning technological lag. The country cannot continue subsidizing, through inflation and lack of competition, an inefficient industrial sector that has proved incapable of generating export revenues, reducing domestic costs and supplying acceptable products for the internal market.

Similarly, the country's system of land tenure needs to be overhauled. Since the revolution, the *ejido*, or system of individual possession and use without ownership, sale or inheritance rights, has played a key role in maintaining social peace in the traditionally violent Mexican countryside. The economic cost, though, has been high; with the exception of cash crops in a few northern and central states, Mexican agriculture and investment in rural areas have remained stagnant for years. This, in turn, has led to a skyrocketing food import bill. From a strictly economic point of view, the obvious solution would be to eliminate the *ejido*, thereby creating a freer market for land, investment and labor in Mexican agriculture. But the political and social costs of uprooting much of the rural population would be astronomical; no government has dared even to tinker with the *ejido*. President De la Madrid's term is probably too advanced for him to have the time for such a major undertaking.

Finally, Mexico's foreign investment laws, which usually require 51 percent ownership by Mexican nationals, will have to be modified if the nation wants to replace foreign credit with foreign equity participation. Since the 1940s, Mexico has been a haven for many multinational firms because it offers a large domestic market, cheap skilled labor, a developed infrastructure and proximity to the United States. But potential investors have been put off by unfavorable changes in what are euphemistically called "the rules of the game" in the 1970s, the unexpected nationalization of private banks by then President José López Portillo in September 1982, and the general uncertainty over the health of the Mexican economy.

Problems with direct investment are complicated because Mexico is now trying to attract a different type of foreign investor: small and medium firms, with high potential for export or transfer of technology, instead of the large firms that have traditionally dominated the local investment scene. The incentives that drew larger companies in the past are insufficient for their smaller counterparts in these troubled times. Mexico wishes to obtain well over $2 billion a year in net currency inflows through foreign investment, but this will apparently only come with major changes in the investment laws. In a July agreement to allow IBM to build a computer plant in Mexico, the government demonstrated flexibility in applying existing legislation by allowing IBM to retain full ownership. Such flexibility, however, will probably not be sufficient to stimulate the desired investment.

All of these reforms, then, have the same drawbacks: they are politically costly, economically destabilizing in the short run, require long lead times, and would tarnish the government's nationalistic, progressive image. The Mexican political system is accustomed to implementing exactly the opposite type of change: politically expedient, economically painless, profitable in the short term, and in accordance with the government's traditional rhetoric. The political cost of each reform is high; the price to pay for all of them could be prohibitive.

The wily Mexican bureaucracy will fight tooth and nail against reforms that would diminish its perks and privileges, as many of them would. Furthermore, the economic modernization entails a social modernization as well. The Mexican labor movement will have to change, and with it labor-management relations. For example, if the corrupt state-run unions are shaken up, the union bosses will no longer be able to guarantee labor peace in the oilfields. Likewise, drastic cuts in the purchasing power of wages, like those imposed since 1982, will probably not be as submissively accepted in the future. No wonder then that the De la Madrid administration has barely begun to move in this necessary but politically uncomfortable direction.

It appears that President De la Madrid will be able to face the political storms arising from these economic reforms only if he also advances on the other economic front: Mexico's foreign debt.

If he is to take the measures that in effect will open Mexico up to the world, the government must also show that it can stand up to foreign bankers, the IMF and the United States. Without such a quid pro quo, Mexicans are unlikely to accept the risks of economic restructuring. And only by drastically reducing the interest payments on its debt will the government be able to finance the growth Mexico needs to make economic reform politically feasible.

Mexico's leaders must perform a delicate balancing act. They must bring debt service down from the current 55–60 percent of export earnings to roughly 25 percent for a fixed and substantial period of time. At the same time, they must not acquire new liabilities (as implied by an interest cap, for example) or destroy the possibilities for fresh foreign credit. Moreover, this must be accomplished with the full support of the international financial powers and without a unilateral cessation of payments, which would force Mexico into autarky and provoke a confrontation with the United States. This dual necessity of both paying less and receiving more will be difficult, perhaps impossible, but certainly no more so than any of the challenges on the domestic front. A lasting solution to the debt problem is an indispensable, though not sufficient, condition for economic and political change in Mexico.

VI

Another obstacle to be overcome is the current state of Mexican-U.S. relations. Traditionally this has not been an item on Mexico's agenda of critical, unsolved problems. Relations have varied over time, depending on the governments and the issues in question. But aside from the endemic asymmetry between the two neighbors, relations have not been a major headache for either country. This has changed radically in recent times.

Today, the problems caused by the Reagan Administration's constant, highly publicized (in Mexico, in any case) and often abrasive insistence on the need for major changes in Mexico's domestic and foreign policies have become one of President De la Madrid's most pressing concerns. Likewise, Mexico's continuing economic crisis and growing political and social difficulties are increasingly at the center of U.S. international preoccupations. Both sides have a point; neither can abandon its stance without risking at least minor damage to its national interests, but one side is more dramatically affected than the other. Obviously, that side is Mexico.

Both sides can readily identify the problems, whether they involve illegal immigration into the United States, drug traffic in Mexico, safety for U.S. tourists, foreign investment laws, trade subsidies or even more abstract questions such as "democracy in Mexico." Many sectors of Mexican society have reached the same conclusions as many Americans regarding the changes needed. But, to a man, government officials, businessmen, intellectuals and journalists in Mexico believe that American pressure—regardless of its immediate effects—not only does not contribute to bringing those changes about but, insofar as it becomes a problem itself, represents an obstacle to significant reform. Very little can be achieved in Mexico without U.S. support, but even less can be done if that support is too obtrusive.

One case in point is the counterproductivity of U.S. efforts to have Mexico abandon its support of Central American and Caribbean revolutionaries. On the one hand, they have brought results: Mexico no longer espouses the cause of revolution in the Caribbean basin, and its once close relations with Nicaragua's Sandinistas have soured. But to the extent that President De la Madrid is no longer viewed in Mexico as the progressive and nationalistic statesman that Mexican presidents are expected to be, he is encountering greater difficulties in making concessions to the United States in other areas, and in implementing domestic and economic policies perceived as conservative and/or pro-U.S.

U.S. pressures are often seen as insensitive or hypocritical. This is because the issues, timing and intensity of American pressure are usually impervious to Mexican political winds and customs. Thus, earlier this year, at a time when Mexico was facing other serious problems, the United States provoked a major confrontation over the murder of a U.S. Drug Enforcement Agency official operating in Mexico. The United States felt that the Mexican government's zeal in pursuing the case was insufficient. Mexico considered Enrique Camarena's death regrettable, but no more so than that of the more than 300 Mexican drug enforcement officials who have lost their lives in the war on drug trafficking.

Mexico is not accustomed to being a center of attention. It has great difficulty in coping with other countries' interest in its own affairs, regardless of the reasons for that interest. Undoubtedly, present U.S. concern, whether expressed at the government level or through the press, is something Mexico will have to adjust to, but this will take time. The extensive and perhaps exaggerated coverage, for example, of the July 7 congressional and gubernatorial elections was totally unprecedented. Never had Mexico's peculiar electoral ways been subjected to such close scrutiny. In the long term, this is certainly good for the country; for the moment, it rubs most of its decision- and opinion-makers the wrong way.

In the last analysis, the United States has an extremely delicate—and in some ways paradoxical—role to play in the unfolding Mexican drama. It must understand, on the one hand, the importance of Mexico to U.S. interests, but on the other hand, that it can do very little to influence positively the course of political events.

There is no longer any question that Mexico is in trouble: its political system is exceedingly tired, if not exhausted; its economic situation will deteriorate further before it gets any better; and relations with the United States will remain tense and complex. The United States would be the first to feel the change if things should get out of hand. Frequently mentioned scenarios of leftward drift, subversion or Central American contagion are all totally irrelevant to the present Mexican situation and strictly a figment of U.S. arch-conservative imagination. The danger is rather one of a breakdown in Mexico's traditional forms of social peace, political stability and economic progress; it could be gradual or precipitous, but there would be no simple antidote.

The United States has significant stakes that would be affected by instability in Mexico. Among the likely repercussions for the United States were such a breakdown to occur are massive inflows of illegal immigrants, fleeing not only depressed economic conditions but political chaos; the endangering of U.S. assets in Mexico, from investment and trade to consulates and other government agencies; and difficulties for the 275,000 U.S. citizens presently residing in Mexico.

Despite these stakes, any American involvement, no matter how disinterested or well intentioned, cannot fail to complicate matters further. If the United States hedges its bets by exploring possible alternatives to the present political system, or peaceful transitions to a new one, it will weaken current Mexican authorities. This will in turn make more likely a breakdown in the system. Granted, standing by passively if the Mexican situation continues to deteriorate also carries risks. In addition to the political cost of such passivity, the United States might well ask itself later in hindsight what would have happened had it acted differently. Nevertheless, there is no U.S. role that would carry more benefits than costs.

There is one exception: on the debt issue, the United States should be ready to help if and when help is requested; American economic aid and support will most certainly be needed in this matter. On issues Mexico regards as primarily domestic, however, the United States should maintain a distance and a policy of strict noninterference in Mexico's political life—however high the stakes, however strong the temptation to advise, suggest or impose.

The bottom line is that Mexico will pull through its present crisis if, and only if, four equally important conditions are met more or less simultaneously. First, Mexico's economic modernization of trade, foreign investment, the state-owned sector, subsidies and land tenure must come about quickly and forcefully. Second, substantial and lasting relief on the debt front must be achieved soon, probably during 1986. Debt service must be limited to around 25 percent of export earnings, in a way that will not irreparably damage the country's future creditworthiness. Third, although Mexico is not a dictatorship, it is certainly not as democratic a nation as its inhabitants want it to be. A profound democratization of Mexico's political institutions and of its social structures is perhaps the demand that most Mexicans want fulfilled. Finally, Mexico must return—and the United States must not impede its return—to a highly nationalistic, progressive foreign policy in Central America and the Caribbean. Mexico has national interests in the area and they must be furthered. By pursuing such a regional policy, Mexico will be strengthened, and thus better able to tackle the other three crucial conditions.

The country that will emerge from its current travail will not be the same as the one most Americans, and all Mexicans, knew before. But it will probably be a better country for all concerned. Before this happens, though, there will be many close calls, instances where appearances and perceptions indicate breakdown and even anarchy. The United States, its government, its press and all those concerned by events south of the border, will need a great deal of calm and steady nerves. But Mexico has found itself at the brink of disaster before, and has always succeeded in stepping back. It can do so once again.

HOW 'LA CRISIS' IS CRIPPLING MEXICO[3]

Mexico's most prestigious daily, *Excélsior*, publishes a magazine of news and commentary every Thursday appropriately entitled *Jueves*. The issue that ushered in 1986 had a grim cover: A poor Mexican—one shoe missing, his clothes tattered, his body beaten and bruised—excitedly waved goodbye to a seer wearing a toga emblazoned with "1985." Behind the unwitting Mexican stood a bully of an infant sporting a sash identifying him as "1986." The infant clutched an oversized club adorned with the greeting, "Happy New Year." The year just passed was difficult for Mexicans, and this one will be equally rough.

From 1940–70, Mexico's economy grew at an annual rate of almost 6.5 percent—a pace surpassed only by Japan and Finland among the non-Communist developed nations and by a few advantaged developing countries, notably Libya, Korea and Israel. The phenomenon was dubbed the "Mexican miracle."

Large segments of Mexico's population were left behind, however, especially rural Indian communities. In 1970, the average urban salary was five times higher than the average rural salary. Indeed, the ability of the rural poor to eke out a living has been

[3]Reprint of an article by Forrest D. Colburn, teacher in the Department of Politics at Princeton University. Reprinted by permission from *The New Leader*, 69:5–7. Ja. 13, '86. Copyright © 1986 by *The New Leader*.

called "Mexico's other miracle." According to the World Bank, the distribution of income here has long been worse than in El Salvador.

Mexico's steady economic growth was nonetheless impressive. Most citizens enjoyed a much more comfortable life than their parents did. And there was at least the hope that the marginal poor could someday be brought into the fold. In addition, Mexico's prosperity brought legitimacy and stability to the political offspring of the Mexican Revolution, the governing Institutional Revolutionary Party (PRI).

Then in 1970, under President Luís Echeverría, Mexico's economy began to unravel. By 1982, when José López Portillo's Administration completed its tenure, Mexico had a 600 per cent devaluation of the peso for the year, a debt of U.S. $85 billion, 100 per cent inflation, rising unemployment, and the first negative growth rate since the Revolution. Although what became known simply as *la crisis* was brought to a climax by falling oil prices and a contracting world economy, its underlying causes were expansionary fiscal and monetary policies that had been designed to ensure growth at any cost (or, as one cynic put it, the spending of oil revenues like lottery winnings), plus the peso's continued overvaluation.

With the folly of his economic policies revealed, López Portillo chose a political solution to save face. In his last State of the Union message on September 1, 1982, he nationalized the Mexican banking system and introduced foreign exchange controls. The startling expropriation of the banks was decreed "in the national interest." They had "betrayed" and "plundered" the country, it was said, by aiding and abetting the *saca-dólares* (individuals who had sent money abroad). But the move could not be justified on economic grounds, even if it did temporarily save López Portillo from public humiliation.

Worried Mexicans and nervous international bankers alike, therefore, looked to Mexico's incoming Administration to end *la crisis*. Miguel De la Madrid assumed the Presidency on December 1, 1982, and quickly committed Mexico to a program of austerity and efficiency tailored by the International Monetary Fund. He pledged himself to reverse the ever-growing government budget deficit, which in 1982 was equivalent to 18 per cent of the country's gross national product (GNP).

The following year, Mexico's GNP declined by 5.3 per cent and inflation was 81 per cent. International bankers were heartened, though, by the reduction of the deficit to 8.5 per cent of GNP. According to preliminary figures, Mexico managed to attain positive economic growth in 1985, while holding the deficit at 9.6 per cent of GNP and bringing inflation down to 57 per cent.

Yet these macroeconomic statistics mask the extent to which Mexico's economic problems have gone from bad to worse. The foreign debt, so alarming at $85 billion, has climbed to $96 billion in three years. More troubling to Mexicans (few of whom believe the debt will ever be paid), though, is their declining real incomes. Wage increases have not kept pace with rising prices of essential goods and services. Last year, for example, they went up only around 39 per cent compared with the 57 per cent general hike in price levels. Announcements by toy manufacturers that their already depressed industry sold 25 per cent less toys during the 1985 Christmas season is merely one of the many indicators that show life still is getting more difficult for middle-class Mexicans.

Furthermore, the statistics available apply largely to the middle class; everything suggests that the poor, who always have had a hard time in Mexico, are now having an even harder time. In fact, there is some evidence that the country's inequitable distribution of income has worsened. A study by an economist at the National University has concluded that average urban salaries are now 6.25 times higher than their rural counterparts.

Many of Mexico's continuing economic problems can of course be traced to the drop in oil prices. Nearly 70 per cent of its foreign exchange comes from oil, and 50 per cent of the government's revenues is derived from the state petroleum company, Pemex. The volume and earnings of petroleum exports fell both in 1984 and 1985. A Mexican economist has predicted that earnings from petroleum will fall another 13 per cent in 1986. His guess as to the precise level of the decline is probably no better than those that are less pessimistic, but the point is no one doubts earnings will slip again.

Mexico recently cut its oil prices and announced it would in the future adjust them on a monthly basis, to stay competitive with the volatile world oil market. More changes may be forthcoming, possibly including an easing of restrictions on the sale of oil to Mexico's principal customer, the United States. (Jealous of its independence, Mexico currently limits single-country sales to 50 per cent of its total production.)

If a significant part of Mexico's economic troubles can be blamed on the international oil market, it is increasingly obvious that the government itself must bear some of the blame as well. De la Madrid, only halfway through his six-year term, is the subject of a new book whose title focuses on his failure to confront the crisis, *El Fracaso de Miguel de la Madrid Ante la Crisis*. The persuasive argument presented by the author, Victor Manuel Cuevas, traces the country's morass to the government's steadily expanding participation in the economy.

Efforts to promote growth through state intervention were initiated during the reign of Luís Echeverría and accelerated by López Portillo. In 1970 there were 86 public enterprises in Mexico. In 1982, before the nationalization of the banks, there were 947 public enterprises. Not surprisingly, this thrust was accompanied by an explosion of government bureaucracies that began undertaking everything from rural development projects to the promotion of popular culture. With the nationalization of the financial institutions, government responsibility increased further: Not only did the state become *the* banker, it assumed responsibility for the myriad of companies that were either partially or totally owned by the banks.

Today the government is by far the largest employer in the country, and according to several estimates accounts for half of Mexico's GNP. Besides owning and managing the all-important petroleum industry, it presides over an eclectic conglomerate consisting of textile mills, most of the movie industry, real estate companies, luxury hotels, lumber mills, sugar refineries, and virtually every other type of business imaginable. It even runs a golf course.

Since the state's involvement to this degree has mushroomed in the last decade or so, there is little systematic information about its efficiency relative to the private sector. Nonetheless, horror stories have begun to emerge that underscore what a white elephant government administration has been. Public enterprises are said to suffer a whole host of maladies: inadequate definition of objectives, poor organization, underutilization of resources, lack of cost control, poor coordination with other government enterprises and bureaucracies. Whispers of corruption also abound. The latest of these cite personal loans to bureaucrats that are many times higher than their annual salaries.

What the state does not run it often regulates, and here too it is accused of promoting inefficiency. The government regulates the prices of basic grains, for instance, and sets them uniformly for the entire nation. Consequently, agricultural producers in areas with higher than average costs, such as northwest Mexico, no longer find it worthwhile to cultivate basic grains. Equally debilitating has been the failure of the expansive Mexican state to carefully and convincingly delineate the respective roles of the public and private sectors. Because it feels the "rules of the game" are not clear, the private sector inclines toward caution rather than risk-taking.

Cuevas and other critics argue that De la Madrid has sought to reduce Mexico's deficit by raising revenues when he should be reducing unproductive outlays. Instead of freeing itself of unprofitable enterprises and unnecessary bureaucracies, they maintain the government businesses boost their prices to consumers where they have a monopoly, as many do. Or else the government raises taxes to shore up undertakings that face competition and to hold together its swollen managerial groups.

International bankers are appeased by this—or any—method of controlling the national deficit. It matters little to them that nothing concrete is happening, that the private sector and the general public are simply being forced to underwrite unrestrained government expenditures. The bankers' narrow interest is whether Mexico lives within its means; the more fundamental issue of the economy's true productivity is not their concern.

Why is Mexico's President pursuing a course that is so patently empty? Ideology may be part of the answer. More persuasive is the view that spreading money around is politically useful.

Mexican politics runs on cooptation, the trading of small favors for allegiance. A big budget means a bigger bag of favors.

Under De la Madrid the private sector has had only one unequivocal victory against the state—the dismantling of the agency responsible for exports, which was in reality hindering the sale of goods abroad. A few public enterprises have been unloaded, but invariably in an ambiguous fashion. A case in point is a company that manufactures bicycles. It was sold not long ago to the powerful Mexican labor union, the Confederation of Mexican Workers. Since the union is allied with the Administration (much rhetoric to the contrary notwithstanding), it is not clear to what extent the firm will be made to stand on its own feet financially.

The President and Finance Secretary Jesús Silva Herzog have pledged themselves to making the public sector more efficient. No one doubts that they would like to fulfill their promise. The trouble is they have yet to figure out how to make the public sector worthy of its cost in a way that would in their view be politically feasible.

Meanwhile, Mexico is going about trying to service its astronomical debt in a period of falling oil prices in predictable fashion. Herzog has already made his first trip to the United States in search of the $4 billion Mexico estimates it needs to borrow in 1986, assuming a precipitous plunge in the value of its crude does not send the figure up to $8 billion. Despite denials, it is hard to believe this is doing anything more than borrowing from Peter to pay Paul—or perhaps merely borrowing from Paul to pay Paul. In the short run there may be no alternative. But if the country is ever to relive the "Mexican miracle," it must put its own economy in order. And that will necessarily entail a thorough revision of the government's business practices, or its getting out of the business of being in business.

MEXICO TIGHTENS ITS BELT[4]

Mexico is a place where worlds come and go, sometimes sinking out of sight. In the 16th century, Cortés obliterated the Aztec culture in one of history's more thorough conquests. But 200 years before that, the Aztecs had built their own civilization near the ruins of an earlier, forgotten people. To this day, Mexicans are haunted by the ever present fear of still another apocalypse, and there is enough bad news in their economy at present to keep the specter alive.

Almost always, it seems, the Mexicans fall into success and then out of it before it does much toward eliminating the country's rampant poverty and underemployment. No sooner had Mexico begun to reap riches from vast new oil finds in the 1970s, for example, than the world's industrial economies became mired in recession, and unneeded oil was squirting out everywhere. Petroleum prices plummeted, deflating the hopes and dreams Mexico had fashioned for itself when it became the world's fourth largest oil producer.

During that bonanza, Mexico added $48 billion to its foreign debt, for a total at present of $85.5 billion, and only last summer it tottered on the brink of national bankruptcy. Now, however, the country appears to be making some headway toward dealing with the debt, which is expected to cost $10.5 billion in interest payments this year alone. The new government of President Miguel de la Madrid Hurtado, which was inaugurated in December, has begun an austerity program aimed at slashing Mexico's huge budget deficit, halting unnecessary government spending programs and slowing its virulent, 116% inflation. If the world economic recovery continues, Mexico may be able to step back from the brink. Says Finance Secretary Jesús Silva Herzog: "The pace of the U.S. recovery, interest rates and the oil market will decide our fate. All we need now is a little luck."

[4]Reprint of an article by John S. De Mott, *Time* staffwriter. Reprinted by permission from *Time*, 121:48-50. Je. 13, '83. Copyright © 1983 by *Time*.

Loan-repayment targets for the first four months of the year have been met, and Silva Herzog says confidently, "Whatever happens, Mexico will live up to its financial commitments." Almost all new money the country gets is going to pay back old debts. Mexico should receive some $12.3 billion in emergency loans from the International Monetary Fund and other lenders this year. Boasts Silva Herzog of recent cash infusions: "Of the $3 billion from new loans since March, the entire $3 billion flowed right back out again to amortize some of our debts and pay interest on others."

Few economies have been jolted so hard, so rapidly as Mexico's. After four years of an oil-induced boom that saw the gross national product grow at an 8% average annual rate, Mexico's economy nose-dived last year when the price of oil fell. This year the G.N.P. may decline by as much as 5%. During the first three months of the year, as the government's austerity program took hold, industrial production was off 11%. Mexico's auto industry, the country's largest non-oil enterprise, suffered a 50% drop in sales. Iron and steel production cooled by 11.5%. The output of radios and other appliances dropped 20%. Even beer consumption was off 20%. The number of jobs in the economy shrank by about 8%, adding perhaps as many as 1.6 million more people to the 10 million already out of work or underemployed in a work force of 30 million.

De la Madrid began the belt tightening by devaluing the peso immediately after taking office. At the same time, he adopted very strict measures to bring down inflation. The goal is an annual rate of 55% by year's end. Consumer interest rates were increased from 40% to 70% per year, gasoline prices were doubled, and a 15% value-added tax was slapped on all but the most essential goods.

The results of the austerity program show up everywhere. Mexico City's shops are bursting with goods, but there are few customers; bored clerks chat idle hours away. Auto showrooms are deserted, and understandably so: a Volkswagen Rabbit sells for 800,000 pesos, more than double the 360,000 of last summer. Ford, GM and Chrysler have stopped including fancy U.S.-made electronics in their Mexican-built cars to get around import restrictions.

↗On the streets, men in tattered clothing water shrubs, scrub public monuments, whitewash scaly tree trunks or sweep nearly empty stretches of roadway gutters. Business has slowed drastically even in places that cater to the rich. At Las Mañanitas in Cuernavaca, a favorite weekend retreat for the capital's elite, stately white peacocks pick their way among sparsely occupied cane lawn chairs. A few months ago, Mexico's well-to-do had to wait an hour to get a table. Says Claudio Weiz, an Argentine businessman in Mexico City: "Mexicans are in a trauma. They have never suffered this kind of crisis."

Many of the businesses still open are deeply in debt. Sales of Rodacarga Co., a maker of materials-handling equipment, shrank from $20 million to less than $5 million as the peso became worth less and less and the austerity program began taking hold. A loan the company has from Philadelphia's Girard Bank now exceeds its entire peso capital. The firm's order backlog, usually nine months, has dropped to four. Company President Carlos Lopez has been forced to close down two of his company's three plants and lay off 362 of his 509 workers.

The squeeze may serve as a warning for countries who once sought quick riches from their natural resources only to find themselves stymied when commodity prices fell. Counting on a permanent high price for oil, Mexico had borrowed heavily from banks in the U.S. and elsewhere to finance drilling, steel production, roads, hospitals and increased automobile manufacturing. Bankers in New York, Tokyo and London dispensed the money after only cursory precautions because the loans were paying lucratively high interest rates of as much as 17%. Moreover, it all seemed so safe. Mexico's oil exports were rising from a paltry 200,000 bbls. daily in 1977 to 1.5 million bbls. in 1982. Last year, in fact, the country surpassed Saudi Arabia as the largest supplier of foreign oil to the U.S.

Then, almost as suddenly as it began, the Mexican "economic miracle" ended. In August, Finance Secretary Silva Herzog announced at a gathering of bankers in New York that Mexico would not be able to make scheduled payments, due over the following 90 days, of more than $3 billion. Weak oil prices had robbed the country of anticipated revenues and left it almost penniless. Says Jorge Chapa, co-owner of a large Mexican supermarket chain: "We were rich at $16 per bbl. of oil, and at $32 we were broke because we spent as if the price were already $36."

Washington, mindful of the $7.2 billion invested by American companies in Mexican enterprise and fearful of economic and political instability on its border, moved in with nearly $3 billion in emergency funds, including $1 billion in advance payments for strategic reserve oil purchases from Mexico, $1 billion in short-term funds to tide the country over, and another $1 billion in credits for such commodities as corn and beans. The International Monetary Fund gave promise of support but in return demanded the austerity program that De la Madrid has put in place.

Despite all the troubles, a few signs are beginning to indicate that the economy may be starting to pick up. At the Bolsa, the Mexican stock exchange, the mood is improving. Analysts there lightly chide each other for being perhaps a little too apocalyptic. "Not all is lost," said one observer, "because of weak demand, lack of investments and sales." Mexican companies, he feels, will just have to learn to live without profits for a while. The Bolsa's stock index, which anticipated the crisis last year and sank to 450 points in August after hitting a high of 1450 two years ago, recently rebounded and closed last week at 1087. Nonetheless, many stocks still sell for only two or three times earnings vs. an average of almost 13 for American companies on the Standard & Poor's 500.

Here and there around Mexico, other signs of an economic upturn can be seen. The clampdown on foreign goods, for example, has worked. Imports are down 70%, running at $4 billion below targets. That has helped create a balance of payments surplus of $3.4 billion vs. a $708 million deficit for the same period last year.

More money is pouring into the country too. Two weeks ago, Xerox officials announced they would be spending $100 million to $150 million on a new manufacturing plant for small copiers, which will be exported to the U.S. Sheraton will build five more hotels to take advantage of the new tourist boom. Americans are now rushing to Mexico to bask in the sun and pick up bargains with their strong dollars. A Japanese consortium is ready to start work on a new 700-room hotel in Mexico City.

Yet even as Mexico tries to hold the line against disaster, its biggest problems remain largely unsolved. Two-thirds of the country's 76 million people live as rock-poor *campesinos* on subsistence farms in some of the worst rural and urban slums anywhere in the world. Undernourishment is widespread. Four of ten Mexicans never drink milk; two of ten never eat meat, eggs or bread. They live mainly on tortillas and refried beans. Some government solutions seem almost pitiful. Coca-Cola and other soft drinks are subsidized to sell for a pittance of 6¢ because their sugar content is considered nutritious.

Nothing seems to go far toward breaking the old Mexican pattern of maldistribution of wealth or bridging the vast chasm between rich and poor. Meanwhile the population keeps growing at a rate of 2 million annually. That increases pressure on authorities to deliver more jobs and social services. It also increases U.S. worries about a tide of illegal aliens.

Right now, one of the few things relieving some of the pressure on the Mexican government seems to be a widespread attitude of *ni modo*, a fatalist mood of "nothing can be done about it." Even labor unions are not optimistic about getting big wage increases. They had been asking for a 50% hike but probably will get only 20% at best, even though inflation has chopped the buying power of the average worker by 60%. Working union members seem happy enough just to have jobs. Two weeks ago, attempts to get a general strike off the ground fizzled. While bankers and economists feverishly work to pay interest on the country's huge debt, politicians and businessmen nervously hope that the present political calm will last.

MEXICAN FOREIGN POLICY:
THE DECLINE OF A REGIONAL POWER?[5]

Riding the crest of the petroleum boom of the late 1970's, Mexico surfaced in the early 1980's as an independent and influential actor in hemispheric affairs, particularly in Central America. The clearest example of the country's growing foreign policy autonomy was President José López Portillo's diplomatic and economic support for the Sandinista revolution in Nicaragua from 1979 through 1982, despite deepening United States hostility toward that regime. Other examples included the Mexican-Venezuelan oil accord of August, 1980; the joint Franco-Mexican declaration on El Salvador of August, 1981; López Portillo's 1982 Central American peace plan (launched in Managua on February 21, 1982); Mexico's critical attitude towards the United States position in the Falklands-Malvinas conflict of April–June, 1982; and the Mexican-Venezuelan joint diplomatic note on the Nicaraguan-Honduran conflict put forward on September 15, 1982. In each case, the Mexican leadership evidenced open foreign policy disagreements with the United States over how to handle regional problems and undertook diplomatic and/or economic initiatives that ran counter to United States policies.

In August, 1982, however, Mexico's five-year economic boom ended in a dramatic financial collapse, a result of falling petroleum prices on the international market, deepening world recession, and unrealistic and poorly implemented national economic development policies involving massive foreign borrowing. Consequently, when President Miguel de la Madrid Hurtado assumed office on December 1, 1982, he inherited a heavily mortgaged and deeply depressed economy teetering on the brink of bankruptcy.

The threat of Mexico's default on its international loan commitments sent shockwaves through the highly exposed United States financial community and precipitated frantic United States

[5]Reprint of an article by Bruce Michael Bagley, author and Assistant Professor of Latin American Studies, Johns Hopkins University. Reprinted by permission from *Current History*, 32:406–09, 437. D. '83. Copyright © 1983 by *Current History*.

government efforts to stave off unilateral Mexican action. Nonetheless, some members of President Ronald Reagan's administration believed that Mexico's economic difficulty contained a silver
lining for the United States: Mexico would inevitably be forced
to adopt a lower international profile and to pursue a less
"adventurous" foreign policy in Central America and the Caribbean because of its lack of economic resources and its increased
dependence on the United States and other foreign creditors. In
other words, the obstreperous Mexicans would be forced to return
to the sidelines of hemispheric affairs and stop undercutting United States policy in Central America.

Neither of these images of Mexico—autonomous regional
power or economic basketcase—fully captures the complex reality
of Mexico's contemporary relations with the international system.
Oil wealth undoubtedly provided Mexico with the additional economic resources and the sense of self-confidence needed to assume
an expanded role in hemispheric affairs in the early 1980's. At the
same time, it was apparent to most observers, including many
Mexicans, that even with oil wealth the country's own economic
future remained inextricably tied to that of the United States.
Mexican authorities could not afford to allow foreign policy dis-
putes with the "colossus of the North" to spill over into, or damage, Mexico's bilateral economic relationship with the United
States. Hence, even at the height of the oil boom, Mexico's foreign
policy autonomy was effectively limited by its continuing economic and technological dependence on the United States, as well as
by its overwhelming military inferiority. In short, Mexico was
never as autonomous an actor in foreign policy as it was sometimes
portrayed to be during the euphoria of the petroleum bonanza. In
fact, throughout the 1979–1982 period, the López Portillo administration was careful to present its various foreign policy initiatives
in Central America as complements or reasonable alternatives to
United States positions, rather than as frontal opposition. Furthermore, the Mexicans expressly recognized United States strategic interests in the region and maintained close communication
with Washington.

The polar image of Mexico as an economic basketcase is similarly flawed because it fails to take into account the complex na-

ture of United States–Mexican economic relations in the 1980's. The extensive, although decisively asymmetrical, interdependence that characterizes the contemporary United States and Mexican economies, especially the heavy exposure of several major United States commercial banks, left the Reagan administration no real alternative but to assume the leadership of the international bailout needed to prevent total economic breakdown in Mexico after August, 1982. In spite of its distress over Mexican foreign policy in Central America and the Caribbean and its disapproval of the López Portillo administration's September 1, 1982, economic emergency policies (bank nationalizations, monetary controls, protectionism, reluctance to accept International Monetary Fund austerity guidelines), the Reagan administration moved quickly to backstop the Mexican economy, because failure to do so would have involved unacceptable costs to American economic interests, including several possible major bank failures and the severe disruption of the entire Western financial system.

Although the United States strongly pressured Mexico to reach an agreement with the IMF and tied much of its bailout aid to United States commercial interests (e.g., International Commodity Corporation credits for Mexican purchases of United States grains, advance payments against Mexican oil deliveries to the Special Petroleum Reserve), the Reagan administration made no overt efforts to link United States economic concessions to modifications of Mexican foreign policy either in Central America or beyond. The United States simply could not risk such linkages (although some in the administration were sorely tempted), because they would have met with intense resistance and might have precipitated a unilateral Mexican decision to default on the country's huge US$80-billion-plus international debt.

The point is that United States–Mexican asymmetrical interdependence cuts both ways. On the one hand, during the 1979–1982 period of oil-fueled expansion, Mexico's relative autonomy within the international system, although certainly greater than it had been, remained limited by the overwhelming importance of its bilateral economic relationship with the United States. President López Portillo had more political-diplomatic clout in the Caribbean Basin than his predecessors because of oil

and the overall growth of the Mexican economy; but the ways in
which this increased influence could be used in Central America
or elsewhere and the degree of effectiveness he could achieve were
still circumscribed by the hegemonic actor, the United States.

On the other hand, the collapse of the Mexican economy has
not meant, as some observers predicted, that Mexican leaders have
lost all foreign policy autonomy or that they have been forced to
modify the basic thrust of their country's policies in Central
America. Whether it liked Mexico's Central American policies or
not, the United States government simply had to support a Mexican bailout. Under the circumstances, linkage strategies were essentially useless; United States leaders could not seriously
threaten to withhold American economic support from Mexico
even if foreign policy concessions were not forthcoming. As a result, during his last crisis-ridden months in office, President López
Portillo continued and even intensified his diplomatic support for
negotiated settlements of the conflicts in Central America, while
simultaneously presiding over his country's tempestuous negotiations with the United States, the IMF and the international banks.
During his first year in office, President de la Madrid pursued a
similarly independent regional foreign policy, despite his country's virtually prostrate economy.

Mexico in Central America

President de la Madrid has demonstrated his government's de-
termination to maintain an independent role in Central America
by actively supporting the Contadora Group's efforts to bring
about negotiated settlements of the conflicts in the region—a policy consistent with the earlier efforts of López Portillo. The first
meeting of the Contadora Group (Mexico, Venezuela, Colombia
and Panama) took place in early January, 1983, when their respective foreign ministers met on the resort island of Contadora
in Panama (hence the name, *Grupo de Contadora*) to discuss the
possibilities of coordinated action to defuse the increasingly explosive situation in Central America. Following a series of encounters
between both Presidents and foreign ministers, the Contadora
Group sponsored a four-point regional peace proposal involving

an immediate cessation of fighting and arms shipments, the withdrawal of all foreign military advisers, the signing of mutual non-aggression pacts by the countries in the area, and the recognition of the sovereignty and right to self-determination of each of those nations.

While the Reagan administration ultimately decided to applaud the actions of the Contadora Group publicly to avoid being labeled as the major stumbling block to peace in Central America, in fact the United States has consistently expressed reservations about the viability of Contadora-style peace initiatives and has systematically ignored or downplayed them. During 1983, the Reagan administration rhetorically endorsed Contadora's search for peace in Central America, while simultaneously financing a not-so-covert war against the Sandinista regime in Nicaragua and increasing military and economic aid to El Salvador, Honduras, Costa Rica and even Guatemala. In September, the United States launched major joint naval-military maneuvers with Honduras, involving one of the largest United States contingents ever assembled in the region, to demonstrate United States support for the Honduran government, to increase United States–Honduran military preparedness in case of an eventual conflict with Nicaragua, and to further "tighten the screws" on the Sandinistas through "gunboat diplomacy." And in October, in a surprising move, the United States invaded Grenada to "forestall a Cuban military buildup" (in the words of the administration).

American rhetoric aside, Mexico and the Contadora Group have confronted an increasingly hard-line and aggressive United States policy. Indeed, within the Reagan White House, Central American policymaking power shifted rapidly in mid-1983 from the "pragmatic" United States State Department and Assistant Secretary of State Thomas Enders to the "hard-line" and staunchly Reaganite National Security Council headed by William P. Clark. While Secretary of State George Shultz was apparently able to win approval for his own choice for the key position of Assistant Secretary (Langhorne Motley, former Ambassador to Brazil) over the more conservative alternatives proposed by the White House staff, the rise of well-known hard-liners like United Nations Ambassador Jeane Kirkpatrick, United States Special Am-

bassadors Richard Stone and Otto Reich, and General Paul
Gorman of the United States Southern Command in Panama to
key advisory positions indicated that the Reagan administration
is not likely to embrace the Contadora formula in the foreseeable
future.

The Contadora Group has sought support for its peace proposals among the Central American countries and the various opposition forces, as well as in the United States Congress and
abroad. Central Americans have generally reacted cautiously to
the Contadora efforts. Members of the United States Congress,
particularly many Democrats, have frequently endorsed the Contadora approach but have been unable to force the Reagan administration to alter its policies or to move ahead with serious
negotiations. In fact, by raising the specter of losing another Central American country to communism (like Nicaragua), President
Reagan has been able to divide the Democratic party and to deflect
much of his domestic opposition in and outside Congress. Finally,
although the Contadora Group has made attempts to invoke the
good offices of sympathetic European leaders like Prime Minister
Felipe Gonzalez of Spain, Prime Minister François Mitterrand
of France, and spokesmen of the Socialist International, the Reagan administration has steadfastly rejected their counsel.

In the face of United States resistance to Contadora and the
intensification of the military dimensions of United States policy,
President de la Madrid adopted a more subdued foreign policy
and leadership style than his predecessor. Within Contadora, Co-
lombian President Belisario Betancur (a progressive Conservative
inaugurated on August 7, 1982) emerged as the most dynamic
leader among the Contadora four. Several hypotheses have been
suggested to explain de la Madrid's lower profile. Certainly his
preoccupation with his own nation's acute economic problems di-
verted time, energy, and resources away from Central America.
It is also clear that de la Madrid was concerned with reducing fric-
tions and establishing a smoother relationship with the United
States.

In this context, the fears expressed by some Mexican businessmen and policymakers over potential United States commercial
reprisals and growing protectionism were believed to have forced

de la Madrid to adopt a more cautious approach. Finally, some commentators have noted that de la Madrid feels less personally committed to Nicaragua and the Sandinistas than López Portillo.

In June and July, 1983, the de la Madrid administration suspended petroleum shipments to the Nicaraguan government because of the Sandinistas' failure to keep up payments on the US$300 million already owed. In light of Mexico's own economic difficulties and its subsequent decision in August, 1983, to renew oil supplies to Nicaragua, however, it appears premature to read into the action any major shift in the country's foreign policy stance.

While de la Madrid may in fact feel less personally committed and more heavily pressured than López Portillo, Mexico cannot afford to be as generous with the Sandinistas as it was in the past. Equally relevant, it almost certainly could not shoulder a similar economic commitment if revolutionary regimes were to emerge in El Salvador, Guatemala or elsewhere in the area. Just as President de la Madrid has been forced to impose severe domestic austerity at home, he has also found it necessary to limit the economic resources his government can commit to foreign policy.

This does not mean, however, that President de la Madrid has "knuckled under" to Reagan administration pressure. There are two basic reasons why he is unlikely to do so. First, to counterbalance his rightward drift on the domestic front and forestall criticism from the Mexican left, it will be politically expedient to maintain, at least rhetorically, a progressive posture in Central America. Second, de la Madrid and his advisers believe that Mexican national interests will be better served by a policy that helps to prevent the widening of the conflicts in Central America and thus the likelihood of even deeper United States military involvement. Indeed, during his August, 1983, meeting with President Reagan in La Paz, Baja California Sur, de la Madrid expressed open disapproval with Washington's announced military maneuvers along the already tension-filled Honduran-Nicaraguan border.

From the Mexican perspective, the Reagan administration's hard-line, military approach is fundamentally counterproductive; it promises to prolong and deepen the region's instability at great cost to Mexico. The most obvious costs for Mexico are represented in the flood of Central American war refugees pouring into the country. Some estimates put the total number of Salvadoran refugees in Mexico as high as 350,000 and the number of Guatemalans at around 100,000. If the wars in those countries continue for several more years, as even the most optimistic of the Reagan administration's pacification scenarios for Central America contemplate, then the numbers fleeing into Mexico will increase. If the United States, directly or through proxies, continues to press the war against Nicaragua from Honduras and Costa Rica, it is only a matter of time until refugee populations from these countries also begin arriving in Mexico.

Less obvious but even more costly to Mexico over the long run is the fact that continuing turmoil and instability in Central America will inexorably force the country's leadership to divert economic resources from development programs to defense (particularly of the vulnerable southern border and oil fields) and will shift decision-making power from civilian to military elites. In the context of the country's already severe austerity program, the additional sacrifices involved in financing a major military buildup could be exacted only through increasing repressive and authoritarian policies.

In light of these perceived threats to Mexico's interests and the political advantages to be gained at home with a mildly anti-American foreign policy, it is highly unlikely that President de la Madrid will abandon his country's efforts to find peaceful solutions to the ongoing conflicts in Central America. Not only do the Mexicans feel threatened by the Reagan administration's bellicose strategy in Central America, they find it difficult to understand the long-term goals or purposes behind the Reaganite approach to the region. Unlike the United States leadership (both Republican and Democratic), the Mexicans have few reservations about dealing with single-party, authoritarian political systems of a socialist and revolutionary stripe. After all, Mexico's Institutional Revolutionary party (PRI) has ruled uninterruptedly for over half a century and continues to wrap itself in the (admittedly threadbare) mantle of the 1910 Mexican Revolution. For Mexico City, the overwhelming foreign policy priority in Central America is to end the fighting and stabilize the region politically and economically in order to avoid disastrous consequences for Mexico.

Like his predecessor, President de la Madrid believes that he can work with (and perhaps even moderate) the leftist revolutionaries in Nicaragua and elsewhere in Central America and the Caribbean. Power-sharing formulas through which the revolutionary left could participate in the governance of the country (and could even assume full control at some future point) are not, therefore, seen as threatening, or at least not so threatening as a widening of the conflict in the region.

In Washington, the principal policy priority is not stability but rather the prevention of further Soviet-Cuban Communist penetration in the Caribbean Basin. Political stability is a prized goal, but not if it comes at the price of another country "lost" to the Soviet Union. The range of regime-types the Reagan administration is willing to tolerate in "America's backyard" does not include socialist or Communist states, especially those allied militarily with Cuba and the Soviet Union. Indeed, rather than seeking an accommodation with the Sandinista regime, the Reagan administration appears convinced of the need to destabilize and ultimately roll back the Sandinista revolution, while preventing similar leftist victories in other Central American countries through stepped-up American military aid and economic assistance.

The fundamental difference between current Mexican and United States foreign policies in Central America lies not in how they explain the origins of the current conflicts (internal versus external) nor in the mechanisms they propose to end the fighting (power-sharing versus elections), although both dimensions are important. The key difference lies in the political outcomes each country is willing to accept or tolerate. President Reagan and his advisers have made it clear that the United States can and will use force (either direct or indirect, covert or overt) to secure outcomes compatible with their view of United States vital interests. The invasion of Grenada is an example of this policy.

Conclusion

President Miguel de la Madrid and the Contadora leaders clearly disagree with the Reagan administration. Their various peace proposals and mediation efforts, although publicly applauded by the Reagan White House, have gone nowhere in the face of systematic United States opposition. Time appears to be running out on Contadora. The tensions between Nicaragua and Honduras have risen to explosive levels as Honduran military complicity in the United States–backed guerrilla war being conducted against the Sandinistas has become evident. Nicaraguan–Costa Rican tensions are also heating up as Edén Pastora Gomez and his ARDE (Revolutionary Democratic Alliance) guerrillas have intensified their activities. The possibility of open warfare between Nicaragua and Honduras looms increasingly large. The Reagan administration is stepping up military aid to the Honduran and the Salvadoran militaries and even to the army-less Costa Ricans. The potential for region-wide conflict in which the United States might eventually become directly involved has never been greater.

The Reagan administration would certainly like to avoid any direct United States troop involvement in the Central American conflict and has repeatedly denied any plans to send American boys to die in the jungles. The recent displays of "gunboat diplomacy" in Honduras were clearly meant to intimidate the Sandinistas into more acceptable behavior (halt arms supplies to El Salvador, restore political pluralism and a mixed economy) and thereby avoid the need for United States intervention. The covert war waged by the United States Central Intelligence Agency is apparently directed toward similar ends.

While Mexico and President Miguel de la Madrid retain sufficient autonomy to maneuver diplomatically through the Contadora Group, the trend toward militarization and confrontation appears to make Mexico and the Contadora initiative increasingly irrelevant to the Central American equation. As political negotiations take a backseat to the force of arms, an economically crippled and militarily weak Mexico appears to have only a limited role to play in the Central American tragedy.

OIL AND POLITICS IN MEXICO[6]

Mexico City's cartoonists have had a field day with their country's hydrocarbon reserves, which have increased over 12-fold to 72 billion barrels in the last decade. Some have depicted *el petróleo* as a guardian angel, fluttering down to save the nation; others have shown it as a new Virgin of Guadalupe, also playing a redemptive role; finally, it has been sketched as black gold, flowing profusely from a cornucopia-like vessel resembling Mexico itself.

These caricatures notwithstanding, the oil has proved a mixed blessing to this ancient Aztec nation of 75 million inhabitants. The highly publicized deposits did attract hundreds of bankers, who literally elbowed each other out of the way to offer the federal government, Petróleos Mexicanos (Pemex), the state oil monopoly, quasipublic agencies, and private corporations loans on increasingly generous terms. "They . . . [had] an almost blind faith in the country's reserves," according to the *Economist* (London). The influx of dollars facilitated the achievement of a key goal of President José Portillo's 1979 Industrial Development Plan: gross domestic product (GDP) grew by approximately 8 percent each year between 1978 and 1981. Pemex drilled scores of new wells onshore and in the shallow waters of Campeche Bay, laid hundreds of miles of gas and oil pipelines, built loading terminals at Dos Bocas and Salina Cruz to handle supertankers, and launched construction of a giant complex to make the country self-sufficient in key petrochemicals. The expansion helped generate nearly one million new jobs annually.

This growth was accompanied by the beginnings of "petrolization"—a neologism connoting an overheated economy fueled by huge oil revenues, growing reliance on foreign creditors to pay for surging capital and luxury imports, a convulsed agricultural sector, and—above all—gaping budget deficits. Rather than raising taxes, Mexican leaders chose to cover the growing deficits by printing crisp new peso notes and borrowing heavily abroad.

[6]Reprint of an article by George W. Grayson, John Marshall Professor of Government, College of William and Mary. Reprinted by permission from *Current History*. 82:415–20, 435. D. '83. Copyright © 1983 by *Current History*.

This action spurred inflation, which fell to 17.5 percent in 1978 only to climb to 18.2 percent in 1979 and 26.3 percent in 1980. Even with slight monthly adjustments via-à-vis the dollar— the so-called "dirty float"—the peso's overvaluation was obvious. A dearer peso discouraged tourism, inhibited the export of Mexican manufactures (some of which were relatively labor-intensive), and exacerbated reliance on oil and its derivatives to earn foreign exchange. Hydrocarbons, which generated 16 percent of Mexico's export earnings in 1976, accounted for over 75 percent of these revenues five years later. Meanwhile, a grossly overvalued peso gave the middle class access to foreign goods and travel on a scale out of reach of their counterparts in many developed states, thus accentuating the debt crisis.

Until mid-1981, most Mexican policymakers believed that oil prices would continue to rise. Higher prices would assure foreign exchange earnings that would continue to propel economic development, while funding illicit payments to hundreds of self-serving politicians, Pemex officials, and union leaders preying on an industry suffused by corruption.

A confluence of factors—record production in Saudi Arabia, conservation measures, reduced consumption, substitution of other fuels in industrialized nations, and expanded output by Great Britain, Mexico, the Soviet Union, Norway, Egypt, and other non-OPEC producers—generated a 2 million to 3 million bpd (barrels-per-day) world surplus in early 1981.

Mexico's attempt to maintain high prices—$38.50 per barrel for its light Isthmus variety crude and $34.50 per barrel for the heavier Maya grade—as the seller's market shifted in favor of buyers sparked an exodus of customers, a sharp decline in export earnings, and a major hemorrhage of dollars. Small and large investors alike increasingly doubted the government's ability to protect the markedly overvalued peso. To help bolster Mexico's flagging economy, President Ronald Reagan's administration purchased 109,000,000 barrels of oil for the United States Strategic Petroleum Reserve (SPR), established to immunize the United States against short-run disruptions in supply. This government-to-government transaction (announced in August, 1981) contrasted with previous purchases for the SPR, which had involved giant oil companies as intermediaries. The sale to the SPR symbolized a more pragmatic policy, which increasingly manifested itself in Pemex's approach to pricing. Market pressures gradually forced price cuts: by late 1982, Pemex was offering Isthmus at $32.50 per barrel and Maya at $25. The latter was especially attractive to fuel oil producers serving the United States east coast, where Mexico was displacing Venezuela in sales.

A further example of Mexico's pragmatism came in a second sale to the Strategic Petroleum Reserve. This $1,000,000,000 deal was signed in September, 1982, as part of a multibillion dollar rescue package to pull Mexico from the brink of bankruptcy. The accord involved a government-to-government sale of approximately 40,000,000 barrels of Isthmus at the extremely favorable price to Washington of $25 per barrel.

Seven months later, Mexico accepted without posturing or diatribes a decrease from $4.94 to $4.40 in the price per thousand cubic feet of natural gas sold to Border Gas, a consortium formed by six United States pipeline companies. As recently as 1979, dismay at the unwillingness of the United States to accept what Mexico perceived to be a fair price for its natural gas prompted López Portillo to administer a tongue-lashing to United States President Jimmy Carter during the latter's visit to Mexico City. An oversupply of natural gas in the United States and Mexico's still relatively high price also led Border Gas to reduce daily imports from 300 million cubic feet to 180 million cubic feet, a move that, coupled with the lower price, cost Pemex $169.1 million in earnings in 1983.

Closer Ties to OPEC

When Mexico pragmatically enlarged its volume of exports during a contracting world oil market, Venezuela suffered the greatest loss. In October, 1982, Mexico surpassed Saudi Arabia as the principal exporter to the United States market. Increased Pemex sales also contributed to the pressures besetting OPEC (Organization of Petroleum Exporting Countries) to lower the price of Saudi Arabian light, the reference crude on which OPEC prices are based. Indeed, at least seven members of the cartel had begun quietly trimming prices, providing discounts, extending the period for payments, tying the crude price to its product yield value, and employing other ingenious methods to sell their oil below the minimum level set by the group.

For obvious reasons, Venezuela and other OPEC members had urged Mexico to join the 13-nation cartel. Mexico, traditionally eager to maintain its freedom of action in international affairs, demurred. Nonetheless, it generally followed the cartel's pricing lead.

A reevaluation of Mexico's oil policy attended the election and installation of a new Chief Executive, Miguel de la Madrid, on December 1, 1982. Before his inauguration, a special "energy committee," one of several transition task forces examining key policy areas, recognized inter alia the need to "avoid conflicts with the rest of the producing companies. . . . " According to its report, it behooved Mexico to

leave open the possibility of entering OPEC and abandon its unilateral policy of isolation that is incompatible with its status as an important world class producer and exporter of petroleum.

Even if it did not affiliate with the cartel, the country should embark upon a "search for new forms of dialogue, cooperation and negotiation with OPEC, with some of its most distinguished members and with non-OPEC exporting countries."

De la Madrid and Mario Ramón Beteta, Pemex's new director general, took these proposals seriously in fashioning an international energy policy. Cooperation replaced competition with OPEC as Mexico explored ways to help stabilize a world petroleum market whose collapse would have dire consequences for its debt-ridden economy. After all, between 1979 and 1982 petroleum consumption by non-Communist nations had shrunk 12 percent to 46 million bpd. During this period, OPEC's share of the market had declined from 31 million to 20 million bpd, and prospects for the cartel appeared bleak in the absence of a commitment to lower prices and establish a new production quota.

In March, 1983, after months of haggling, the OPEC members reaffirmed a decision reached a year earlier to limit their combined output to 17.5 million bpd and to adhere to a lower benchmark price of $29 a barrel. Producers promised to refrain from both discounting prices and producing more crude than their assigned quotas.

Although not a party to this accord, Mexico followed the negotiations carefully. From February to mid-March, Pemex held off quoting prices to buyers, awaiting action by the cartel. High representatives of the Mexican government attempted to keep abreast of market developments in meetings held with counterparts from Venezuela, Algeria, Saudi Arabia, Nigeria, Norway and Great Britain in advance of the London negotiations. During that conference, Mexican officials in the British capital kept in close touch with the OPEC ministers.

Moreover, in the aftermath of the agreement, Mexico brought its Isthmus price ($29) into line with OPEC charges and announced the continuation of a 1.5-million bpd export ceiling during 1983 for reasons of "long-term interest." As Beteta and Energy and Mines Minister Francisco Labastida expressed it:

In spite of [Mexico's] current situation of excess demand for Mexican crude, we will continue to hold to this export target. In today's delicately balanced market, any attempt by a large exporter to maximize foreign exchange revenues in the short run increases the risk of a similar action by other exporters that also require additional foreign exchange. Eventually, such behavior could affect the current price level. This would imply a further reduction in foreign exchange income for oil exporters.

President de la Madrid learned first hand about Pemex when he served as director of the monopoly's finances in the early 1970's. He knew of the firm's major strength—well-trained, dedicated engineers, a noteworthy research and development capability and the most sophisticated structure of any oil company in the third world. He also knew of its weaknesses—rampant feather-bedding, waste, profiteering and malingering.

As a result, he brought in Beteta, an outsider with a reputation for honesty, to shape up Latin America's largest corporation. A 55-year-old lawyer and economist, Beteta had held a series of high-level government posts: under President Luis Echeverría, he had served as Treasury Minister (1975–1976) and under López Portillo he had headed the Banco Mexicano Somex, a government-run institution that encourages, funds and even manages industrial ventures.

Beteta took the reins of Pemex at a time of retrenchment. A belt-tightening program hammered out with the International Monetary Fund (IMF) probably reduced the GDP by 3 to 5 percent in 1983. Meanwhile, Pemex found itself strapped for funds as price reductions lowered the firm's export revenues from all hydrocarbons to $14.5 billion, down from $16 billion in 1982. Pemex's budget for 1983 was $6.5 billion, a 42 percent reduction in real terms over 1982. The new director general faced the challenge of maximizing physical and financial yields from the monopoly's existing installations, while completing only high-priority projects like the huge La Cangrejera petrochemical complex on which work was well under way. The cutback forced Pemex to stack drilling rigs, postpone expanding some refineries and pipelines, and lay off over 10,000 employees from a distended payroll of 120,000.

Just to keep its 2.7-million bpd output, Pemex had to earmark $2 billion for new wells in all major fields already in production, including Cactus, Samaria and Canduacan, to compensate for declining yields from existing wells with falling reservoir pressures caused in some cases by the use of improper management techniques during the previous administration.

Maintaining production with fewer resources was a task that paled in comparison to Beteta's assignment to combat corruption in the oil sector. De la Madrid had vowed to push "moral renovation," the anticorruption theme that he trumpeted from Chihuahua to Quintana Roo in his electoral campaign. This concept aroused tremendous interest because the ubiquitous corruption affects everyone—from the equipment salesman required to pay a kickback to the company purchasing agent to the taxpayer incensed by ex-President López Portillo's moving into an ostentatious five-home compound on 7.5 acres outside the capital. "It doesn't matter if they steal a bit," said a taxi driver inured to forking over *mordidas* or bribes for real or fictitious traffic infractions, "but they shouldn't steal so much."

De la Madrid has begun his drive where they do steal "so much": the oil sector, which generates three-fourths of Mexico's foreign exchange and where corruption and chicanery abound. Each new Mexican chief executive vows to put the government's house in order just as his United States counterpart regularly pledges to balance the budget. Of course, neither promise is fulfilled. Yet de la Madrid knows that he must husband every peso available to revive a limp economy. Politically, a spirited, well-publicized crusade that sends a couple of "big fish" from the last administration to jail would raise his standing now that his ever so brief honeymoon with the Mexican people has ended because of his no-nonsense application of a stern stabilization plan.

Placing Beteta at the helm of Petróleos Mexicanos represents an encouraging sign of presidential interest in reforming an industry that had become a dollar-filled trough of peculation during the previous administration. For instance, Pemex constructed a $1.5-billion gas pipeline from the Isthmus of Tehuantepec to the Texas border when the enlargement of one or two existing lines and the addition of several connecting lines could have accommodated the flow at a fraction of the cost. Similarly, Pemex constructed a 50-story-plus skyscraper at its Mexico City headquarters complex when decentralization of economic activity was a stated priority of the López Portillo regime. It would have been vastly less expensive to have erected five 10-story buildings than to have built the "Pemex Tower," especially in view of the abundance of land owned by the monopoly. In a January 21, 1982, speech, Beteta warned that "while I am director . . . immoral deals will not be made in the shadow of the largest national industry." Two months later, he stressed that

our industry belongs, not to the petroleum workers alone, but to the nation as a whole. Intelligent management and proper usage of our resources must favor Mexico, and our basic objective is to serve the community and not to benefit the individual.

The real test of the anticorruption drive is whether it takes on the 120,000-member oil workers' union (STPRM), which is in a class by itself when it comes to shady activities. A wide array of charges have been leveled against STPRM's leaders by former union officials, by the leader of the National Petroleum Movement (a reformist element within STPRM), by scholars, and by investigative reporters for such publications as the magazine *Proceso* and the daily newspaper *Excelsior*.

While nominally it is just another labor organization, the union and its 29 locals not only boast an effective political apparatus but also hold business interests in posh hotels, oil drilling concerns, construction companies, huge farms, credit unions, supermarkets, hospitals, swimming pools, gymnasiums and funeral homes.

Nobody begrudges the union the right to amass wealth and influence. But evidence is accumulating that this wealth has been built on activities which, in many cases, have taken money from the pockets of rank-and-file workers to enrich union big shots. For example, under its contract with Pemex, the union recruits virtually all nonmanagement employees of the oil monopoly. Union officials often take a "bite" out of the checks of the estimated 13,000 "aviators," people who don't work but show up to collect their wages on payday anyway. Retired workers may be obliged to labor on union farms or risk the loss of their pensions. A petroleum engineer hands over thousands of dollars to the union for a lifelong position; and temporary secretaries sometimes pay for their jobs with sexual favors.

Pemex channels 2 percent of all its investments to the "social works" of the union. This contribution totaled $220 million between 1976 and 1982. Undeniably, much of this money went to projects that benefited union members, like housing, sports complexes, schools, and health clinics. However, some critics question whether all these funds are directed to the projects.

The press in Mexico City regularly comments on the affluence of senior union officials, including their fondness for large homes, private airplanes, jewelry, and trips to the gaming tables of Las Vegas. How union officials accumulate such wealth has never been documented in detail, but it is known that some top officials wield great patronage influence through companies formed in the name of their locals in activities ranging from pipe manufacturing to construction. Such firms allow union officials to take advantage of a Pemex concession, first granted in 1977, awarding the union 40 percent of all onshore drilling contracts.

According to reports, this enabled the companies belonging to the union locals to subcontract the drilling work and pocket handsome commissions. In some places, like Poza Rica, union companies collected commissions from Pemex on wells that were needlessly drilled. The stakes in the Pemex-union drilling deal can be seen by the fact that Pemex spent nearly $4.5 billion for onshore drilling between 1977 and 1981.

Drilling contracts are centralized in the union-dominated National Commission of Contracts, headed by Joaquín Hernández Galicia. Known by friends and foes alike as "La Quina," a childhood diminutive of his first name, Hernández Galicia is the real power behind STPRM, although he has not been its elected director since 1964. He continues to place his loyalists, like current union president Salvador Barragán, in key union posts.

One of La Quina's bitterest enemies and critics is Hebraicaz Vázquez Gutiérrez, who founded the National Petroleum Movement in the early 1970's as a reform element within the union. Vázquez, who had served as a local union official, claimed the union uses some 3,000 armed men on Pemex's payroll to repress dissidents and whip up support for union ventures. Vázquez's efforts at reform ended in failure and he was subsequently arrested on a charge of being involved with a guerrilla movement and jailed. Since his release, Vázquez has been unable to get his job back with Pemex, but his friends have sent petitions to the new Mexican government requesting his reinstatement.

Why hasn't the government cracked down on the "petroleum jungle," as journalists describe the oil industry? To begin with, labor is the sturdiest pillar of the ruling Institutional Revolutionary party (PRI), and the oil workers energetically mobilize funds, crowds and votes for favored candidates at all levels. An ability to deliver support won La Quina easy access to the presidential palace under López Portillo.

Moreover, displacing La Quina and his disciples might only bring in a new generation of STPRM leaders, every bit as self-serving as their predecessors but not as devoted politically to the PRI. Investigations of the union could also reveal further peculation within Pemex itself.

De la Madrid claims to be up to this Herculean task, as evidenced by his appointment of the outspoken Beteta. Yet fear of strikes and other dislocations in this pivotal sector raises doubts that sweeping actions will soon complement Beteta's tough words.

The new director general is already suspect for having loaded Pemex's executive offices with highly paid, inexperienced confidants from the Banco Mexicano Somex. Nonetheless, Beteta is smart, hardworking, close to the President, and with a reputation for honesty both in Mexico and among international bankers; and four months after taking office, he threw his weight behind the successful removal of La Quina–backed officers in Local 43, a small maintenance unit, and their replacement by a slate endorsed by the rank and file. Even more significant, the government has indicted Senator Jorge Díaz Serrano, head of Pemex during the last administration and "architect" of the oil boom, for participating in a $34-million fraud in connection with the monopoly's purchase of two Belgian natural gas tankers in 1980.

President de la Madrid seems to have decided that taking up the fight will advance both his political interests and the interests of his country. To pull his nation from the brink of bankruptcy, he needs all the economic resources at his disposal. That means slicing through the inefficiency, bureaucracy and corruption that holds back the Mexican economy.

His campaign is more than just an interesting political sideshow; it is central to Mexico's future. Not only does corruption divert resources from needed modernization, it also instills cynicism among workers. They see that payoffs and the right connections are more important in getting ahead than hard, honest work. This in turn nourishes their alienation from the political system and adds to the enormous strains already besetting it.

San José Accords

Austerity has affected the "Economic Cooperation Program for Central American Countries," commonly known as the joint facility or the San José Accords, after the city in which the agreement was signed on August 3, 1980. This bold plan represents the first collaborative aid effort between an OPEC and a non-OPEC country. Under its terms, Mexico and Venezuela each pledged to ship up to 80,000 bpd of oil on concessionary terms to the five Central American nations plus Panama, Jamaica, Barbados and the Dominican Republic. The exporters promised to grant the importers credits amounting to 30 percent of the commercial price of their purchases for a period of five years at an annual rate of 4 percent. Should the resources derived from these credits flow to "economic development projects of priority interest," notably those spurring domestic energy production, the loans could be extended to 20 years at 2 percent yearly interest, with a five-year grace period. These credits were offered at a fraction of the commercial rate; for instance, the Eurodollar interest rate at that time was approximately 10.5 percent. With donor approval, all countries of the area, including Cuba, were eligible to join the program, which could be renewed annually after an initial one-year period.

Mexico and Venezuela would supply the needs of recipients equally, although shipments of petroleum would be made in accordance with commercial contracts entered into bilaterally by Mexico and Venezuela and the individual purchasing nation. Moreover, an effort would be made to export the oil in ships operated by the Multinational Fleet of the Caribbean (NAMUR), which was set up in 1975.

Even after the agreement was approved, Venezuela tried to convince Trinidad and Tobago to become the facility's third donor. Instead, the island oil producer announced formation of its own loan plan for the 11 members of the Caribbean common market. Between 1980 and 1982, Trinidad and Tobago pledged $208 million to pay the incremental costs of oil, fertilizer and asphalt for the program. In fact, economic considerations at home and political problems abroad limited allocations under this scheme to approximately $75 million.

Caracas and Mexico City renewed the San José Accords in 1981, 1982, and 1983. The second and third renewals were especially impressive because of the serious economic problems afflicting both countries, whose foreign exchange earnings have declined because of falling oil prices. The donors still grant five-year loans automatically. Yet the criteria for the 20-year credits have been altered to emphasize priority development projects or those that promote regional economic integration.

Belt-tightening in Mexico and Venezuela did lead to a modification of the facility in August, 1983. The maximum volume of oil supplies by each nation remains 80,000 bpd; however, the rebate has fallen from 30 to 20 percent of the commercial price. This change leaves the value of concessional aid essentially intact because of the $5.00 per barrel price drop in 1981. The donors also hardened the terms for the five-year and 20-year credits.

Despite the 50-50 supply provision, Mexico failed to match Venezuela's shipments during the first two years. In fact, Mexican exports averaged only 37,925 bpd, 47.4 percent of its 80,000 bpd target in the first year. The two donors have shared the load more equitably since August, 1981, and in 1983 Mexico supplanted Venezuela as the dominant exporter.

Mexico and Venezuela agreed to provide half of each recipient's imports. In fact, refinery conditions and propinquity have dictated that Venezuela would become the exclusive supplier of Barbados and that Mexico would be the sole exporter to Belize should the former British colony seek oil. This postage stamp–sized nation became the tenth beneficiary member of the facility in August, 1982.

Ships for NAMUR have yet to be acquired, possibly because of the unfavorable economic conditions affecting tanker owners in the early 1980's.

The San José Accords have encountered problems. To begin with, virtually all the region's refineries were equipped to accommodate lighter Venezuelan crude, not Pemex's heavier Maya grade. Hence, in the early months, some countries found themselves with an excess of heavy fuel oil and had to import gasoline and diesel from elsewhere. Adjustments in handling capabilities were expensive and time-consuming and, until they could be made, the Dominican Republic and other countries insisted that Venezuela either furnish all their oil or, at least, pre-treat the Mexican crude so that it could be handled in local refineries. This consideration, combined with Venezuela's status as the traditional supplier to these markets, accounts for Mexico's relatively modest exports during the facility's first year. Most recipients have long since made the necessary refinery modifications or blended Mexican and Venezuelan crude to permit processing. Moreover, the bulk of oil shipped by Pemex is now Isthmus, not Maya. Financial distress has caused Mexico and Venezuela to lay aside plans for the possible joint purchase, leasing, or construction of one or more refineries to process their crude for ultimate shipment to facility participants and other purchasers.

Expanding the scope of the program has also posed a challenge to Mexico and Venezuela. Cuba, which depends on the Soviet Union to provide over 95 percent of its oil on cut-rate terms, has never applied for membership; Belize has yet to sign a contract with its oil-rich neighbor; and a 1981 experience with Haiti, which failed to live up to its contractual obligations, proved disastrous.

More serious than membership questions has been the recipients' difficulty in designing projects that would qualify for long-term credits. One of the curses of underdevelopment is an anemic planning capacity complemented by a shortage of engineers and technicians. An inability to devise appropriate projects meant that, as of mid-1982, Venezuela had granted only five of these long-term loans, while Mexico had authorized none.

Awarding long-term loans has posed an increasingly difficult challenge to Mexico and Venezuela, both of which are starved for dollars with which to conduct trade and meet payments on their foreign debt, which exceeds $110 billion between them. In Venezuela, 1983 is a presidential election year, and criticism of foreign aid at a time of domestic distress by business groups and the Confederation of Venezuelan Workers, the nation's major labor organization, forces temporary suspension of Venezuelan long-term credits under the facility in March. Mexico vowed to continue extending concessionary loans.

Attractive terms aside, most beneficiaries have not kept up their payments for petroleum acquired from the suppliers. Nicaragua has failed to pay for any oil received from Mexico. (Venezuela halted shipments to Nicaragua in August, 1982, after the Managua regime missed payments on two deliveries.) In mid-1982, Mexico refinanced an $80-million oil debt that Costa Rica had contracted. Even so, Mexico assured the San José government that it would guarantee oil supplies to Costa Rica for the next three years and would continue financing oil explorations. And the Dominican Republic proposed sending molasses that could be converted into sugar to cover its bill with Mexico.

Might the program be sacrificed on the altar of economic necessity? Despite misgivings by an array of business, labor and bureaucratic groups in Venezuela and, to a lesser extent, in Mexico, termination seems unlikely because the scheme has accomplished goals important to the two nations. It has (1) provided resources to countries that run chronic balance of trade deficits with the donors, (2) encouraged energy nationalism through government-to-government accords in the oil sector, (3) promoted economic stability—or, at least, militated against instability—in a region afflicted by civil strife, (4) offered relatively developed states anxious to avoid revolution an opportunity to influence, if not moderate, the actions of Nicaragua's Sandinistas, (5) demonstrated that Latin Americans can help each other without Washington's involvement, (6) enhanced the donors' international prestige by providing foreign aid with "no strings attached," (7) emphasized that political problems spring from continuous economic crises suffered by small, energy-dependent nations, and (8) embedded a vital stone in a mosaic of international cooperation.

As the donors revise their terms, the recipients must emphasize conservation, intensify exploration for domestic energy supplies, and become more proficient—in cooperation with the Inter-American Development Bank, the World Bank, and other international lending agencies—in fashioning development projects that will merit funding by this extremely innovative facility.

López Portillo's administration squandered billions of dollars of hydrocarbon earnings before de la Madrid took office. Still, Mexico has greatly increased its proven reserves, built an impressive infrastructure in its oil sector, and embarked upon an extremely generous joint facility to aid ten Caribbean basin states. The world oil glut and Mexico's subsequent need for large-scale United States and international assistance to avoid bankruptcy have injected a rare element of pragmatism into Mexican energy policy. Meanwhile, de la Madrid's unflinching adherence to an IMF stabilization program, his assault on corruption in Pemex and its union, and a judicious oil marketing policy coordinated with OPEC may enable Mexico not only to recover economically, but to enlarge its role as a regional leader.

MEXICO'S DEVELOPMENT DILEMMA[7]

Until the summer of 1982, Mexico was riding the crest of a growth wave that rested on newly discovered petroleum wealth and a vigorous government program for comprehensive development. Suddenly the economy felt the shock of a major financial crisis that forced the government to devalue the peso sharply, suspend payment on a massive foreign debt, and cut back severely on its ambitious global plan to turn the nation's nonrenewable oil resources into sustained industrial growth. Public surprise at the abrupt change of fortune was keen, and disappointment grew as the magnitude of the crisis was revealed.

The administration of President José López Portillo, which had benefited from the oil boom and launched the Global Development Plan, was in its last months as the economy began to fall apart. The government took emergency measures, but it fell to the new regime of Miguel de la Madrid Hurtado, who took office as elected President in December, 1982, to cope with the crisis and try to carry on a positive program. The administration's task was similar to President López Portillo's, who at the beginning of his term in December, 1976, had to repair the financial wreckage left by the outgoing presidency of Luis Echeverría Alvarez.

Mexico was apparently setting a pattern, in which each six-year presidential term, or *sexenio*, was characterized by a period of economic exhilaration, followed by a major crisis that confronted the incoming administration with a need to pedal backward furiously before resuming a forward path. In other countries, like Argentina, similar situations have been called "stop-go cycles" when abrupt shifts in policy have played havoc with long-term growth objectives.

The government of President de la Madrid currently faces a major dilemma. In order to overcome the financial crisis and prove to foreign banks and international lending agencies that it is putting its house in order, the government has had to impose severe

[7]Reprint of an article by James H. Street, Professor of Economics, Rutgers University. Reprinted by permission from *Current History*. 82:410–17, 437. D. '83. Copyright © 1983 by *Current History*.

restrictions on consumption, limit credit for industrial expansion and agricultural recovery, and increase the heavy burden of unemployment—in short, to emphasize austerity. However, as coauthor of the Global Development Plan inaugurated by the previous administration in April, 1980, President de la Madrid is committed to the long-term growth and development of his country, and this objective requires expansive policies not permitted by monetary and fiscal restraint.

Moreover, when Mexico returns to the growth path, the government will have to choose whether to continue to shield domestic industry behind protective walls of tariffs and other import restrictions, or to concentrate on competitive efficiency and promote the export of manufactured goods. The choice will be hard because economic recession and the inability to repay privately incurred debt has left Mexican industry in a weakened state.

The de la Madrid administration faces basic questions. How can it surmount the present financial crisis, and at what social cost? And how can the country return to a growth track, and under what long-range development strategy? Before these questions can be answered, deep institutional and cultural failings in Mexican government and business must be corrected.

Paradoxically, Mexico's present dilemma, which it shares with many other developing countries, would probably be less severe if the nation had not had exceptionally good luck in finding unanticipated oil resources soon after the onset of the world energy crisis in 1973. When the Organization of Petroleum Exporting Countries (OPEC) suddenly quadrupled the world price of petroleum in October of that year, Mexico was still a net importer of petroleum products. Proven oil and natural gas reserves were estimated in 1974 at no more than 5.8 billion barrels, but by the next year Mexico had become an oil-exporting country and by 1981 newly discovered petroleum deposits had increased the nation's proven reserves elevenfold to 72 billion barrels.

Petróleos Mexicanos (Pemex), the government's petroleum monopoly, met the challenge of rapid expansion of oil extraction and by 1981 was able to achieve a rate of production of 2.74 million barrels a day. Refining capacity was doubled during this period and petrochemical production tripled. Mexican oil exports rose to 1.5 million barrels a day, about half of which went to the United States. Although there was much waste of natural gas in the extraction process, Pemex contracted in 1979 to deliver 300 million cubic feet of gas a day to a consortium of six United States pipeline companies.

Among nations with large known petroleum reserves, Mexico now ranks fourth, and it is also the world's fourth largest producer. In 1980, Mexico displaced Venezuela as the fourth largest supplier of oil to the United States.

Revenue from foreign sales of oil and gas expanded enormously, reaching $3.8 billion in 1979, $9.5 billion in 1980, $13.8 billion in 1981, and $16.1 billion in 1982. While the increase in export earnings came with great rapidity, the Mexican government repeatedly overestimated its anticipated resources in setting its annual budgets. When the international market for oil weakened in the summer of 1981, the López Portillo administration was obliged to trim spending based on an expected export revenue for 1982 of $20 billion; the final budget counted on only $16 billion. Revenue for 1983 was forecast at another $16 billion, but in March the government reduced its estimate to $13 billion, still high by standards prevailing before the world energy crisis.

The rising income flow permitted Mexico to recover rapidly from the financial debacle inherited from President Luis Echeverría Alvarez's government in 1976, and provided a basis for financing the new Global Development Plan. Moreover, ready lenders from abroad swelled the volume of dollars, Japanese yen and European currencies available for investment and increased consumption. The Mexican government and its virtually autonomous agencies, like Pemex, and giant private financial-industrial combines, like Grupo Industrial Alfa, engaged in an orgy of borrowing from foreign commercial banks, the International Monetary Fund, the World Bank, and the United States Treasury and Federal Reserve System, with the result that current spendable income far exceeded current earnings from exports. In 1970, at the beginning of the Echeverría administration, Mexico's external debt, both public and private, was estimated at about $6 billion. By the end of the *sexenio*, in 1976, the total foreign debt had quintupled to $30 billion.

Under the López Portillo government, foreign borrowings continued to rise; by the inauguration of President de la Madrid in December, 1982, the combined external debt was variously estimated at from $80 billion to $85 billion, of which more than $70 billion (increased by the nationalization of private banks in September, 1982) represented obligations of the federal government. Since the end of 1978, Mexico has ranked second among the developing nations of the world in the size of its external debt, threatening to surpass Brazil. The following year nearly two-thirds of Mexico's exports earnings were required to service this debt.

The Global Development Plan

After a two-year struggle to stabilize the economy after the 1976 recession, in March, 1979, President López Portillo announced a National Industrial Development Plan that was to become the first phase of a Global Development Plan elaborated a year later. The industrial development plan was designed to reduce the excessive concentration of manufacturing in three centers, the Valley of Mexico, Guadalajara and Monterrey, and to stimulate growth in eleven regional development zones throughout the country. Even though unemployment and underemployment, normally high in a country with a rapidly growing population, had been intensified by the economic recession, the government chose to emphasize the establishment of basic industries in preference to labor-intensive enterprises. It was anticipated that by creating new opportunities on the northern and coastal borders, as well as at interior locations, the industrial development program would arrest the flow of migrants from rural areas to the principal cities and would thus take the pressure off the government to provide urban services.

The early phase of the industrial development program did generate a considerable increase in employment as many new industrial projects were undertaken at scattered locations. Since the Mexican labor force has been increasing in recent years at about 800,000 workers per year, new construction was an important element in the boom period.

Partly to achieve cost savings, but also to diversify its sources of foreign investment and decrease its reliance on United States know-how, Mexico turned to Japanese firms to provide much of the basic technology for large-scale construction. With varying degrees of vigor, four new "industrial ports" were begun, at Tampico and Coatzacoalcos on the Gulf of Mexico, and at Lázaro Cárdenas and Salina Cruz on the Pacific coast. Early in 1981, the Mitsubishi Company began a $150-million dredging and harbor construction project to enlarge the port at Altamira-Tampico, and the Kobe and Sumitomo steel companies were awarded contracts totaling $96 million for the installation of a tube mill and foundry at Lázaro Cárdenas. Other Japanese firms were given orders to build petrochemical plants at Tampico and Coatzacoalcos. In addition, the Nissan Motor Company announced plans for a $200-million expansion of its Datsun plant at Cuernavaca. Japanese investment in Mexico reached a historic high of over $600 million in 1981 and continued to expand in 1982.

Canadian firms were also invited to invest in Mexico as an offset to continued dominance by subsidiaries of United States corporations in mixed foreign and domestic enterprises. During this period, Canadian companies invested in a silver mine in Zacatecas, provided telephone switchboards for the Alfa industrial group, and supplied the Mexican electrical system with technology for the long-distance transmission of high-voltage current.

An important part of the Industrial Development Plan was the expansion of the state petroleum industry. President López Portillo repeatedly emphasized the principal objective of the plan was to convert the nation's nonrenewable hydrocarbon resources, which would ultimately become depleted, into a sustained, diversified growth program that would allow Mexico to produce most of its own consumer goods and create a surplus of manufactures for exportation. He warned that the process must not be accelerated too rapidly, for fear of afflicting the country with "economic indigestion" from a flood of oil revenue that would generate inflation.

The President originally set a limit of 2.25 million barrels a day (mbd) as a goal or "platform" for petroleum production that would provide the financial means for industrial expansion and a vast program of social assistance, while still conserving the basic resource. By March, 1980, however, he was persuaded that rising domestic demand for oil products required a 10 percent increase in oil production if export goals were to be maintained. Jorge Díaz Serrano, director general of Pemex, urged that the production platform be raised even higher, to 4 mbd, but by 1981 the accumulation of an oil surplus in depressed world markets meant that Mexico could no longer sell all the petroleum it intended to export without accepting a cut in prices.

During the period of rapid expansion, investment in the petroleum sector was given first priority. In anticipation of revenues, Pemex borrowed heavily abroad to acquire necessary drilling and refining equipment and to broaden its base of operations in the petrochemicals field. European and United States bankers became concerned that Pemex was floating too many loans at prevailing peak interest rates without giving the international financial community time to evaluate the growing risk represented by Mexico's exploding foreign debt.

In the meantime, pressure to expand oil exports persisted, as trade between Mexico and the United States grew by more than 60 percent in 1980, and the Mexican trade deficit increased correspondingly. Imports in all forms exceeded the total value of petroleum exports in that year by about $7 billion. While maintaining commercial oil shipments, in September, 1981, Mexico entered a long-term agreement with the government of the United States to supply the latter's strategic petroleum reserve at rates of 200,000 barrels a day until the end of 1981 and 50,000 barrels a day thereafter through August, 1986. Prices were to be adjusted quarterly.

Earlier concerns about the need for conservation and the dangers of rapid expansion of oil and gas exports were lulled when President López Portillo announced on September 1, 1981, that Mexico's proven hydrocarbon reserves (including both oil and natural gas) had reached 72 billion barrels and that total "potential" reserves were calculated at about 250 billion barrels. Despite warnings by national leaders that Mexico was becoming "petrolized" and committing the same error of "boom and bust" that had been seen in Iran, Venezuela and Nigeria, the public perception grew that Mexico had unlimited wealth. A heady rise in levels of consumption among the urban upper and middle classes soon converted what was to have been a steady but gradual growth process into a raging consumer extravaganza.

The Rural Assistance Program

Despite prosperity in the cities, a vast number of poor farmers in the rural villages who grow mainly corn and beans for their own subsistence saw few benefits from the oil boom. Their lot has been made harder in recent years by a series of severe droughts that have sharply reduced farm incomes and threatened people in many zones with mass starvation. The drought of 1979 so drastically reduced domestic supplies that the Compañía Nacional de Subsistencias Populares (Conasupo), the government's food distribution agency, increased its imports of foodgrains to 11 million metric tons in 1980, 2.5 times the volume imported the previous year. By September, 1980, the cost of food purchases from the United States reached $2 billion, and the government placed large orders for grain and other foodstuffs in the United States and Canada in succeeding years.

In response to the critical food problem, in March, 1980, President López Portillo announced a program he called the Sistema Alimentario Mexicano (SAM) to increase domestic agricultural production. The program set bold targets to achieve self-sufficiency in corn and bean production by 1982 and in rice, wheat, soy beans, and sorghum by 1985. In addition to stimulating output through credit and technical assistance, the SAM program was intended to improve levels of nutrition and raise money income among the small subsistence farmers who constitute the majority of Mexico's agricultural producers.

At an estimated cost of about $4 billion for the final three years of his term, President López Portillo's Global Development Plan included an extensive social assistance program to deal with rural poverty under an agency known by its acronym, Coplamar. This agency was given the task of constructing health clinics, sanitary water systems, local food outlets and feeder roads to alleviate the social and geographic isolation of the rural poor and bring them into a market economy.

While extremely costly, the rural assistance programs represented the government's attempt to reduce the inequities of the oil boom, since Mexico lacks an effective graduated income tax or an adequate social security system to redistribute income.

The Global Educational Program

When the Global Development Plan was announced in April, 1980, it elaborated an exceedingly ambitious goal—2.2 million new jobs in all sectors of the Mexican economy between 1980 and 1982. Since the energy and manufacturing sectors could not be expected to meet more than a fraction of this goal, most of the job creation effort would have to be carried out in the agricultural, construction and service sectors.

The plan projected a need by 1982 for 264,000 additional professionals with graduate training, 220,000 technicians with undergraduate degrees, and 1,526,000 skilled workers of all types. However, the great majority of Mexican adults remain functionally illiterate, especially in poorer regions. The National Council on Science and Technology estimated that in 1975 nearly 70 percent of the Mexican male population over 30 years of age, the bulk of the labor force, had not completed four years of primary schooling.

The educational task was therefore staggering, and the Secretariat of Education was charged with rapidly expanding a vocational training program designated as CONALEP, and with augmenting the fields of university instruction under the newly announced Plan for Higher Education.

The Disintegration of the Development Program

While critics of the Global Development Program regarded it as wildly unrealistic in its short-term aspirations and charged that it relied too much upon a federal bureaucracy not noted for efficiency or honesty, at least the plan sought to direct the nation's newfound oil wealth to constructive uses and singled out for attention most of the major deficiencies in the national pattern of production and consumption.

Nevertheless, ominous signs of failure began to appear during the boom years. Consumers in the urban areas went on a buying spree long before Mexican industry was ready to produce the desired goods. Shopping centers were filled with foreign wares, and contraband trade, particularly across the northern border with the United States, reached record levels. Nearby cities, like Houston, El Paso and Los Angeles, became magnets for Mexicans with dollars to spend, and many wealthy Mexicans invested in luxury homes along the Texas coast, in cattle on the United States side of the border, and in dollar securities.

Inflation, which the government had succeeded in bringing down to a rate of 17 percent in 1978, began to rise again. In 1981, the consumer price index increased by 28 percent, and during the following year prices leaped another 99 percent. The increase in the cost of living was most acutely felt by the urban poor, who were shocked to learn on August 2, 1982, that overnight the government had raised the price of corn tortillas and bread, essentials of every Mexican's diet, by 100 percent. Later in the year, to reduce the cost of food subsidies, the government again doubled the price of these staples.

Dismayed by the indications that his program was crumbling, López Portillo reacted to public criticism and made frequent speeches denouncing speculation, bureaucratic inertia, and corruption within his own government. Yet he lacked effective fiscal controls, and it was apparent that a considerable part of the revenue of the state oil monopoly was finding its way into private hands. Well-publicized increases in the national debt burden and the deficit in the current account (foreign trade and services) led speculators to apply pressure to the peso, and there was a large flight of capital from the country. Many industrial firms hoarded dollars rather than commit them to investment because they feared a devaluation, and their hesitancy slowed the development program.

Events moved swiftly in 1982 as the economic crisis mounted. On February 17, 1982, the Banco de México withdrew support for the peso, which had been stable throughout most of the López Portillo *sexenio*, and its value dropped precipitously by about 45 percent. Private companies with large dollar obligations were hard hit by the devaluation because these obligations now required nearly twice as many pesos to pay off. At the same time, industrial labor unions pressed for wage increases to offset inflation. When the government granted increases ranging from 10 to 30 percent by official decree, many companies refused to pay, saying that they faced bankruptcy. In April, 1982, Grupo Industrial Alfa, Mexico's largest industrial conglomerate, suspended payment on $2.3 billion in debt, including $2 billion owed to foreign banks, many in the United States. In August, Alfa refused to pay even the interest on its dollar debt, which by then amounted to $1.2 billion.

Rumors began to circulate that the Mexican government would also be unable to meet payments on its debt, and a massive flight of dollars from the commercial banks followed. Threatened with the loss of its monetary reserves, the government had to devalue the peso again, and on August 5 it established a dual exchange rate—a floating rate for most transactions and a preferential rate for such crucial imports as food and interest payments on the foreign debt. The floating rate quickly plunged about 35 percent, from about 49 pesos to the dollar to 75 pesos. Shortly thereafter, the government imposed exchange controls for the first time that severely limited access to their bank deposits by holders of dollar accounts. Many business firms and Americans living in Mexico were shocked to discover that they could liquidate their deposits only with heavy losses. A black market rapidly emerged in which dollars could be obtained only at a cost of 150 pesos to the dollar.

In desperation at the continued outflow of dollars, Finance Minister Jesús Silva Herzog turned to the United States government for emergency assistance and received $2 billion in credits, half in the form of advance payments by the Department of Energy for oil purchases for the Strategic Petroleum Reserve, and half in a loan from the United States Commodity Credit Corporation toward Mexican purchases of grain. Other negotiations were conducted with foreign commercial banks to postpone payment of $17 billion in short-term debts, and the Bank for International Settlements, a consortium of central banks, was persuaded to lend $1.85 billion in emergency credits.

This remarkable bail-out operation was to be supplemented by an additional $3.9 billion to be provided by the International Monetary Fund (IMF) over a period of three years. The Mexican government requested this assistance with particular reluctance, since President López Portillo had taken great pride in retiring a previous loan from the Fund incurred at the beginning of his regime. The IMF loan, when it came in December, 1982, was accompanied by strict conditions imposing austerity on the newly installed government of President Miguel de la Madrid Hurtado, intensifying restrictive measures that the López Portillo administration had already begun.

Unable to stem the hemorrhage of gushing monetary reserves, on September 1, 1982, López Portillo took the unexpected action of nationalizing all the country's private banks and placing their operations under government control. With the banks, the government acquired a major interest in many private enterprises partially owned by the lending institutions.

While President López Portillo blamed the banks for permitting and even encouraging the capital outflow from the country, foreign investors were alarmed by the sudden change in the government's attitude toward private property, and new investments virtually came to a halt as confidence evaporated.

President-elect de la Madrid was reported to have disapproved of the government's drastic action in nationalizing the banks, and it was expected that he might reverse the action after he took office. When, however, his administration began to compensate the former owners with government bonds a year after the takeover, it was evident that the banking system would remain under state ownership and control.

Revelations in the last year and a half of the López Portillo administration appeared to confirm rumors that had long circulated about massive corruption in Pemex and other state agencies, as well as in private firms dealing with the government. An investigation by the United States Department of Justice under the Foreign Corrupt Practices Act led to the arrest by the Mexican Attorney General of two former high-ranking Pemex managers and four Mexican business executives on charges of arranging "kickbacks" amounting to $45 million to Pemex officials in return for contracts to sell oil equipment.

Throughout his campaign for the presidential election, which took place in July, 1982, the candidate of the Institutional Revolutionary Party (PRI), Miguel de la Madrid Hurtado, inveighed against corruption in the government, which was controlled by his own party. After his election, he continued to call for "moral renovation" as a major objective of his new regime. Many close observers of Mexican government and business administration shared the view that the traditional custom of the *mordida* (bribe) and the kickback had done much to undermine the Global Development Plan, and that appeals for moral renovation alone would do little to correct these practices.

The impact of the financial crisis of 1982 on the Mexican economy was extremely severe. The annual growth in the gross domestic product, which had exceeded 8 percent in each of the boom years 1979, 1980 and 1981, collapsed to no growth at all in 1982, and was expected to decline by 2.5 percent in 1983. A rough estimate was that one million people had lost their jobs by mid-1983, when the official unemployment rate (probably a gross underestimate) was given as about 8 percent. Meanwhile, countless Mexican citizens fled across the United States border in search of better opportunities.

Border towns were devastated in their normal trade relations after the collapse of the peso in August, 1982. Mexicans accustomed to buying household appliances and other consumer goods on the United States side of the border found their pesos nearly worthless, and Americans with dollars cleaned out food stores in Ciudad Juárez, Nuevo Laredo and Tijuana while Mexicans found that even in their own country their pesos were eaten up by inflation. Consumer prices virtually doubled in 1982, and increased another 48 percent in the first seven months of 1983.

Before he became President, Miguel de la Madrid, López Portillo's hand-picked candidate for the succession, had served as a "technocrat" in the Banco de México, in the Finance Ministry, and as Minister of Planning and Budget. In the latter role, he was regarded as the principal architect of the Global Development Plan, and it was therefore assumed that he would return to the implementation of the plan as soon as possible after taking office in December, 1982.

However, his first tasks were to cope with the grave emergency facing the government in its worst economic recession in 40 years. He imposed a draconian austerity program, with deep cuts in government spending, social subsidies, and consumer goods imports, and raised prices on a number of basic food products, as well as on gasoline, electricity, and telephone service. Consumption taxes on luxury goods were also raised.

For the fourth time in a year, the peso was devalued, and both the preferential or controlled rate and the floating rate were reduced in value by about half. In the open market, a dollar cost six times as much in pesos as it had a year earlier, a change that created nearly insuperable problems for business firms and others trying to meet dollar obligations.

All major public construction projects were suspended, and shortly thereafter the government announced that the SAM program to achieve national self-sufficiency in food production and improve nutrition among the rural poor had "disappeared." Yet as concern grew about rising unemployment and unrest among organized workers, the government announced in January, 1983, that it would spend $2.7 billion to create from 500,000 to 700,000 new jobs in rural areas and in critical poverty zones in the cities. The semiofficial confederation of Mexican Workers (CTM) had remained remarkably passive during the steady deterioration of the economy, but with social hardships likely to intensify throughout 1983, it was expected that public protests would grow.

On May 30, 1983, the de la Madrid regime presented its own National Development Plan for the period 1983 to 1988. Although the plan ran to 412 pages and set out four broad goals for the *sexenio*, it was disappointing in its lack of detail and description of concrete measures to achieve its objectives. The goals announced were: (1) to conserve and reinforce democratic institutions; (2) to overcome economic crises; (3) to recover the capacity for growth; and (4) to initiate qualitative changes required by the country in its economic, political and social structures.

The plan promised the elimination of inflation and monetary instability, reduction of the government's share in national expenditures, protection of employment opportunities, and a vigorous promotion of production, with a greater role for private enterprise.

Echoes of the Global Development Plan could be heard in calls for industrial decentralization, production for export, and increased social equity, but how these aims were to be achieved was not clear.

The National Development Plan was received by the Mexican public with jaundiced interest, since so many national plans had been offered with heavy fanfare earlier. Critics pointed out that until the government could get its house in order and until a really serious campaign was launched to reduce the massive corruption and administrative inefficiency in the bureaucracy and the parastatal enterprises, there was little chance that Mexico could return to a growth track.

While the Mexican government expected a dollar inflow of about $13 billion from oil and gas exports alone in 1983, about 40 percent of the national budget had to be reserved for servicing the external public debt. So long as an immense foreign debt hung over the economy and the nation had to rely on continued special financial assistance, in which the role of the International Monetary Fund was crucial, the government had no alternative to austerity.

The basic dilemma for the de la Madrid government is how to plan for the expansive development necessary to relieve unemployment, hunger and shortages of goods, while practicing the austerity dictated by conventional monetary and fiscal policy. Farther down the road, the nation will have to choose between a protectionist policy of maintaining high-cost industry and limiting imports, or promoting more efficient enterprises that can compete effectively in world markets. Unlike many other developing countries, Mexico is fortunate that it has exceptional resources with which to make these choices, provided that they can be marshalled with greater care.

THE SHAME OF MEXICO[8]

Wealth has impoverished Mexico. Three years ago, as oil gushed from new wells in the country, José López Portillo, then President, asked Mexicans to prepare themselves for prosperity. The reality today is different. Squandered and looted, Mexico's oil wealth has paralyzed agriculture, immobilized industry, destroyed the rural environment, heightened unemployment, and raised the foreign debt to $85 billion—which the insolvent country cannot pay.

Only the power elite has been enriched. Some $40 billion—almost half the foreign debt—has been withdrawn from Mexico by the triarchy that runs the country—politicians, high-level technocrats, and labor-union bureaucrats—all connected to the ruling Institutional Revolutionary Party (PRI). Much of the other half of the foreign debt was invested in oil-drilling equipment, much of which lies rusting in the ports of London or Amsterdam, or in a field in Houston, Tex., for which Pemex, the state oil monopoly, pays a monthly rent of $160,000.

Mexico's peso, once known for its stability, has been devalued by 1,200 per cent since 1976, when departing President Luis Echeverría broke the exchange rate of 12.5 pesos to the U.S. dollar that had prevailed for more than twenty-two years. Today the dollar is worth 150 pesos.

The illusion of abundance, which three years ago evoked demagogic confidence from Mexico's rulers, has given way to rancor. Last April President Miguel de la Madrid, in office barely four months, asked his predecessor López Portillo to leave the country for his personal safety. Hours later López Portillo and his wife flew to New York and Paris in a private Boeing jet owned by Carlos Hank González, former mayor of Mexico City. Meanwhile, in the blue waters off Acapulco, the transoceanic yachts of the former president and the former mayor received orders to sail to the French Riviera.

[8]Reprint of excerpted article by Flavio Tavares, freelance contributor to "O Estado de S. Paulo" of São Paulo. Reprinted by permission from *World Press Review*, 30:26–28. Ag. '83. Copyright © 1983 by *World Press Review*.

Mexico's economic ills began to build years ago, but they were hidden by rhetoric and paternalistic welfare measures. The oil wealth gave new impetus to corruption, an old leech on the Mexican system. It also broadened civil liberties. Press freedom grew, political repression decreased, and the governments of Luis Echeverría and López Portillo enacted tenuous reforms that permitted opposition political parties.

This open climate also allowed corruption to flower. Under López Portillo everything was done quite overtly. He built himself a lavish estate—four houses, an observatory, and a library—occupying the equivalent of twelve blocks in Mexico City. The main mansion resembles a medieval fortress. The ex-President's wife bought a villa in Acapulco with its own beach and dock.

Mexico's most notorious scandal was a mixture of comedy, tragedy, and impunity: the disappearance of 317 million barrels of oil from Pemex tanks in 1977–78. When the press exposed the scandal two years ago, Jorge Díaz Serrano, then director of Pemex, said, "We produce so much that a lot of it evaporates or is spilled."

Besides the millions of barrels of oil that "evaporated" and the millions of dollars paid for equipment that never reached Mexico, Díaz Serrano is accused of diverting almost 94 billion pesos—then worth about $4 billion—from Pemex's treasury in 1979. In 1981 he left Pemex to run for the Senate as a candidate of the ruling PRI, and today he is one of the barons of that house. [In June the Mexican government charged Díaz Serrano with defrauding Pemex of $34 million.]

About a hundred companies serving as intermediaries in purchasing oil-drilling equipment sprang up in Mexico over the past decade, even though Pemex has a division for this purpose. These companies, basically, were offices for the "legal" receipt of bribes and kickbacks.

From government corruption and currency speculation to development programs, everything was calculated in barrels of oil. With the world's fifth-largest proven reserves, the Mexicans threw themselves into the exploitation of their black gold.

From 900,000 barrels daily that the country exported in 1977, the figure grew to more than two million in 1981–82. Mexico's peso was overvalued, and dollars became cheap. It seemed less costly and easier to buy things overseas than to produce them at home.

It also was more profitable to buy stocks or real estate in New York than to invest in Mexican companies. Politicians and businesspeople, rich from oil-related deals, put their wealth in Paris, Switzerland, New York—and Colorado. Large segments of Vail and Aspen, elegant ski resorts in that state, are now Mexican-owned. A Mexican commission to investigate the problem of capital fleeing the country discovered, in the real estate registers of New York City and the South, the names of 11,000 Mexican property owners—almost 80 per cent minors. In mid-1982 the international price of oil went down. It was the beginning of economic chaos for Mexico. Its vaults were empty; it did not have enough dollars to make the payments on its foreign debt. In August the U.S. granted an emergency $3-billion credit, $1 billion represented as advance payment for Mexican oil. Something that the Mexican people had not known was now revealed: the massive debt.

President Miguel de la Madrid has been able to reschedule most of the debt. "The world's bankers continue to show confidence in Mexico's economy and government," observes Secretary of the Treasury Silva Herzog. But the Mexican people have lost their confidence. Its economy strangled by the fall in oil prices, Mexico has little else to sell to the world except coffee, vegetables, and a few manufactured items.

The most optimistic official figures indicate that Mexican oil exports will bring in $15 billion for 1983. Agricultural exports will bring, at most, $5 billion, and tourism an additional $1 billion, for a total of $21 billion. By tightening belts and buying only necessities from overseas, Silva Herzog plans to limit imports to $15 billion. That should leave the country with a $6-billion surplus, but debt service this year will reach $12 billion—meaning a shortfall of $6 billion.

There are other problems. Mexico's neglected agriculture is on the verge of collapse, and the planned purchase of 8,000 tons of grain to feed the population may rise to 11,000 tons. The nation also must import $14 million in industrial parts and supplies if production and employment are to be kept at present levels.

Countless workers, fleeing the unemployment and poverty of rural Mexico, head north to the U.S. every year. Hoping for a job "over there," they resort to many means to cross the border, all illegal. Heladio Ramírez López, director of the National Peasant Confederation, reports, "Between two and three million Mexicans work in the U.S., and about 750,000 cross the border every year to look for work."

This represents a safety valve for Mexico's government. Emigration on such a large scale eases the domestic pressure of joblessness. Once in the U.S. the emigrés find work quickly. Farmers in Texas, New Mexico, Arizona, California, and Georgia prefer Mexicans because they work hard and as illegals they can be underpaid and are not included in Social Security.

Their hardships begin even before they leave Mexico. Gangs of "specialists" charge $500 per person to transport them over the border—hidden in cars, crammed into trucks with false bottoms, or concealed in loads of farm products. Many are soon arrested and sent back to their homeland.

Corruption dominates Mexican life. In 1981, when the oil boom was making high officials rich overnight, 244 members of Mexico City's Transit Police, in a signed statement, alleged that their superiors extorted from them to force them to extort from the public. They said that the police chiefs charged 15,000 pesos for the use of each department motorcycle; 4,000 pesos for each police uniform, which the state theoretically provided free; and another 1,500 pesos for a ticket book and a police revolver. In addition, motorcycle police were obliged to pay 50 pesos a day to their chief inspectors.

Then there are the major union leaders. All Mexico trembles before the power of Fidel Velázquez, a former milkman who has led the Confederation of Mexican Workers (CTM) since 1941. He is the ruler of the union mafia that controls the government party apparatus, manipulates the workers, wields influence over private business, and is a direct beneficiary of corruption at the highest levels.

The CTM is an official organ of the ruling PRI party; its member unions are the only labor organizations recognized by the government. It is they who bring 500,000 Mexicans to demonstrate in front of the National Palace with banners and shouted slogans whenever the government believes it needs a display of popular support. The system is simple: Workers who do not demonstrate risk losing their jobs.

Virtually every leader of every union tied to the PRI has amassed a personal fortune. Officials own factories or stores, or sit on the boards of large companies, meanwhile continuing to serve as labor leaders. Fidel Velázquez, however, is not among them. Twice a senator and a past member of the lower house, he is austere and discreet in his personal life, which may explain why he is the power behind the scenes.

With more than 150,000 members, the oil workers' union is a state within the state. For years its workers, from truck drivers to technicians, could get jobs only by paying the union's leaders. During the oil boom the union quit charging new workers for jobs and began to make even more money other ways: It received—automatically—payment for 40 per cent of all new wells drilled. Smuggling, using tankers that return to Mexico empty, is another way the mafia makes money.

The labor mafia also functions in other large unions and, in practice, controls all strategic sectors of the economy. In 1972 entire trains were derailed on a railroad whose director would not permit the "usual" bribes to union leaders. There has been a single union for electrical workers since the government destroyed an independent one by closing major power plants at which it had organized a majority of the workers. Almost all the major union leaders are rewarded with posts in the Senate or lower house.

Mexico's present state of poverty was not caused only by the scandalous administration of José López Portillo. Mexicans who seek to understand their country know that its high levels of corruption, foreign debt, unemployment, inflation, and industrial and agricultural stagnation are the result of a process that for years has been eroding a political system established in the name of the 1910 Revolution, which cost one million lives—then 10 per cent of Mexico's population.

During his six years in office López Portillo was more like a king than a president, as were his predecessors and as Miguel de la Madrid soon may be, however unwillingly. The Mexican presi-

dency is characterized by the omnipotence of the chief executive—
who can serve for only one six-year term. To remain revered and
seemingly infallible, the president confers privileges, gifts, and
benefits. He rewards adulation by giving budgetary autonomy to
his Cabinet ministers and other key people, thus perpetuating his
power and enabling top bureaucrats to be increasingly ostentatious.

The state is central, "but the respective chieftains are sovereign
in the matter of theft," an old anthropologist says bitterly. The
system is a monarchy with a time limit; the emperor and his vas-
sals change every six years. The ruling party is the palace,
crammed with crown princes who serve in rotation. Political loyalty has the same duration as the presidential mandate.

Administrative discontinuity helps to explain Mexico's internal difficulties. All the actions of a government have a lifespan of
six years, after which they are abandoned. For example, just beyond the majestic pyramids of Teotihuacán, some thirty miles
from Mexico City, a huge reinforced-concrete bridge hovers in
mid-air, alone, without an access road. It was begun under the
previous administration, and the new administration is not inter-
ested in completing it.

President de la Madrid is trying to carry out a "program of
moral renovation of society." He is encouraging new legislation
that will punish corruption, but has encountered problems. Many
of his aides believe it is unfair for him to end the game of corruption just when their turn has come to exploit it. There has been
a reform of the Penal Code; illicit enrichment is now punishable
by fourteen years' imprisonment and by confiscation of the cul-
prits' assets. In approving the reform, however, the Mexican Congress revoked a law that punished "inexplicable enrichment."

"That means an amnesty for all the high officials of previous
administrations who cannot explain how they got rich so fast," explains Adolfo Aguilar y Quevedo, president of Mexico's bar asso-
ciation. Among those who might have been indictable for
"inexplicable enrichment" are former presidents Echeverría and
López Portillo, former Mexico City mayor Carlos Hank
González, and former Pemex director Díaz Serrano.

A new development in recent years has been a university-spawned technocracy composed of inexperienced youths who cut their teeth in the offices of old PRI politicians and capped their careers by taking graduate courses abroad. Most of them do not know their country or understand its problems. They are the children of the old PRI bureaucracy, theoretically modernized.

It is they who now decide economic questions in Mexico. They constitute two large, friendly groups who vie for power without having any major disagreements: the group educated at Yale versus the group educated at Harvard. In this tug of war, says a Mexican humorist, the people prefer the promises of yesterday to today's reality.

MEXICO: WHERE 'LA MORDIDA' IS KING[9]

It was noon in the Mexican desert. Bobby Stone was driving down Highway 57 when a carload of Mexican federal policemen drew alongside. Flashing their badges, they told him to pull over. Minutes later Stone lay hogtied to a cactus tree as the federales *took turns raping his 53-year-old wife, Freda. As they left, one of the cops spat at her the word* "chingada," *an obscenity that summons up the worst horrors of violation. "Why would something horrible like this happen to us?" said Mrs. Stone. "We loved Mexico."*

What has happened to this country that so many Americans are learning not to love? Week after week new stories of violence and corruption perplex with their horror and their scale. Outrages against Americans attract attention, but they only exemplify Mexico's own deep malaise. Americans are quick to condemn but slow to understand this country that is so close to us and so far away.

To get closer, I recently spent five weeks working my way from the border of Mexico City and back. On the way I visited Brownsville, Texas, to hear the Stones' story. Across the Rio

[9]Reprint of an article by Rod Norland, *Newsweek* staffwriter. Reprinted by permission from *Newsweek*, 106:44–48. Ag. 12, '85. Copyright © 1984 by *Newsweek*.

Grande in Matamoros that night, I reminded myself that one rape cannot be the measure of a nation. Yet that final curse made it seem more than just an ugly crime by cops who were never prosecuted. The theme of violation has run through the folklore, argot and literature of Mexico. Over centuries welling up with helplessness, frustration and rage, the exploited have become exploiters in turn. Today many Mexicans describe their police as public predators, their government as an agency for economic plunder and their country as a place rich in resources but doomed to poverty.

Mexicans are also quick to remind us that we look at Mexico through a mirror that reflects the standards of our own more prosperous society. Nonetheless, here is a country sitting on one of the richest puddles of oil in the world—and it's so broke it can barely pay the interest on its overextended loans. A nation that prides itself as a democracy is run by a political party that almost always wins—or, as critics charge, steals—elections. Once again last month the government party made a virtual sweep of local and state elections—and the opposition cried foul. Corruption in Mexico is breathtaking—and not just in its multibillion-dollar drug-smuggling industry. The past president of Pemex, the state-owned oil monopoly, is awaiting trial for having allegedly boodled $34 million in a single ship-purchase deal. The former police chief of Mexico City, Arturo (El Negro) Durazo Moreno, built two homes worth millions of dollars on a cop's pay. "This must be the richest country in the world," runs a popular Mexican joke. "We have 80 million thieves, and they haven't been able to steal it all."

Even Mexicans who tell such jokes would not want to tar everyone with such a broad brush. But Western diplomats say almost offhandedly that they suspect that top officials made off with many billions of dollars during the six-year administration of former President José López Portillo, who is now said to be in Europe. "That's hard to believe, but then look what they say Durazo stole, and he was only the chief of police of Mexico City," says one diplomat. López Portillo has never been charged, and a spokesman refused to comment on the allegations against him.

When President Miguel de la Madrid Hurtado took office at the height of Mexico's economic crisis in 1982, he proclaimed a war against corruption, firing thousands of policemen and prosecuting some corrupt officials. De la Madrid says his campaign has "advanced significantly." The government has seized Durazo's Mexico City palace and turned it into a "museum of corruption." It is also seeking his extradition from the United States on charges of tax evasion. The campaign has been earnest, but it has only brushed lightly at a problem that deeply sullies the Mexican psyche. "*Qué chingón!*" said a Mexican at El Negro's lost palace recently. Literally "What a rapist," the expression really means, "What a man!"

Mexicans call it la mordida *and consider it a national institution. The first time "the bite" was put on me, it was almost convenient. Illegally parked on a nearly deserted curb at the Mexico City airport, my car was promptly hooked up to a police tow truck. The policeman explained that one merely had to pay the "fine" of 2,000 pesos on the spot and the car would be put down. I paid the fine and demanded a receipt. "If you want a receipt," the officer explained, "we'll have to tow the car."*

Bribery is easier and cheaper than a visit to the pound, one of the reasons the bite is widely accepted. Even the new broom in charge of Mexico City's police, Gen. Ramón Mota Sánchez, seems inured to the problem: "[The police] can't be an island of purity in . . . a society like ours." Later an officer put the bite on me for making a legal left turn, and another officer wanted to be paid for helping me find a lost rental car. Soon you find yourself asking, once the bite begins, where does it end?

Reputed drug kingpin Rafael Caro Quintero could answer that: it doesn't. Mexican and U.S. authorities say that by 29 he had built a half-billion-dollar fortune, not just by growing thousands of acres of marijuana but by buying off police and officials on a grand scale. Last November, at the urging of U.S. authorities, Mexican police seized more than $1 billion worth of marijuana from a Caro Quintero plantation in Chihuahua that employed 7,000 pickers. "Do you think a state government wouldn't know about this?" asked an official of the U.S. Drug Enforcement Administration. Later, when accused of complicity in the murder of

U.S. Drug Enforcement agent Enrique Camarena Salazar, Caro Quintero was detained at the Guadalajara airport. But, say Mexican officials, he merely had to write a check of 60 million pesos ($270,000) to Jorge Armando Pavón Reyes, a first *comandante* of the Federal Judicial Police, and the federales let him fly. (Pavón denies the charge; Caro Quintero was captured last April and is awaiting trial.) Some U.S. officials suspect that drug protection goes all the way to the upper tiers of de la Madrid's government. "I am aware that some people have said that there are political levels involved," President de la Madrid said. "[But] Mexico is under the rule of law and cannot act on mere suspicion."

Mexico is the fourth largest oil producer in the world. And yet one oil-industry analyst and diplomat said that it is still largely true that Pemex is "the only oil company in the world that can't make a profit." That has changed now, said Pemex head Mario Ramón Beteta, maintaining that the book profits of the company have increased twelvefold since he took over 2 ½ years ago.

The progress suggests how much may have been stolen before. Twenty-five Pemex officials are subject to criminal prosecution—including the former head, Jorge Díaz Serrano, who insists he is innocent. Many have been charged, but never arrested. In the middle of a boom, the company went $20 billion into debt. Reformers accuse leaders of the powerful oil workers' union of raking off $1.6 *billion* from union funds, a charge the leaders deny. "Cleansing a large house always takes time, and has to be done gradually," said Beteta, whose appointment was the first significant step in de la Madrid's moral-renovation campaign.

Mexico does have its reformers. The day I arrived in Cuernavaca, Gov. Lauro Ortega Martínez had just fired his attorney general and the entire state police force—for the second time. When Ortega took office in 1982, he had tried to stamp out corruption in the state police, hiring new officers from throughout the country. By this spring the new force had become so hopelessly corrupt that he called a meeting and denounced them as "arbitrary, despotic and dishonest." "We don't want to say that all of them were corrupt, assassins, rapists and traitors, but many were," said state secretary Hernando Rojas Arévalo.

Many visiting Americans have learned about Mexican corruption the hard way. In the Pacific-coast resort of Puerto Vallarta, I found myself standing next to musician Stevie Wonder in the airport snack shop as he bought two Cokes. A young woman clerk counted out his change. "He's blind, isn't he?" she said loudly in Spanish. As a friend helped him toward a taxi, he halted a moment and wondered aloud, "Does it really cost $7 for two sodas?"

Petty ripoffs are the least of the problems in Puerto Vallarta. From September through May, Americans there suffered at least 15 burglaries, 24 armed robberies, 54 muggings and thefts, 6 rapes and 1 murder—and those are just the reported cases. State and municipal police say they have never heard about some of the most notable recent assaults—including a case in which 15 Americans on a horseback tour were robbed en masse and later warned by police not to report the case to the local U.S. consul. Or about the sniper at a golf course who shot an American woman dead and wounded her husband before robbing them. Or about a woman who was raped in the bathroom of a restaurant. Although her alleged assailant was arrested, he was released a day later when the tourist returned to the States rather than prosecute. State police officer Enrique Gómez Aguilar said he never heard of the case. "Most rapes aren't really rapes," he said. "There's so much free stuff here, why rape?"

Like many Mexican policemen, Gómez talked about how hard life has become since the peso crashed to less than a tenth of its old value. Now a cop makes about $200 a month, which doesn't go far in a pricey resort town like Puerto Vallarta. The result, said Gómez casually, is that much of the common crime in the city is committed by municipal policemen. (The municipal police say the same of state police.)

Mexican officials point out that although nearly 5 million tourists visit Mexico annually, the U.S. Embassy officially listed only 51 unsolved major crimes against tourists from 1980 through 1984. But the embassy list is a small fraction of the total. Most tourists who run into the Mexican police system find it wise to just leave. Consular offices routinely receive letters from tourists who have returned to the United States, complaining of rapes, robberies and assaults—but since the victims have left, no action can be taken.

The U.S. ambassador to Mexico, John Gavin, has raised the possibility of warning Americans not to travel to Mexico, but Washington so far has refrained from doing so. Instead, it has cautiously praised Mexico's efforts to improve protection for tourists, particularly on the country's woolly highways. "I don't know about the North Americans," said one Mexican politician. "They're here only a couple weeks at a time. But I'm fearful of the highways in Mexico 365 days a year."

The pressures within Mexico have led to a rise in political unrest, mostly along the border. Matamoros is one of those border towns the ruling Institutional Revolutionary Party (PRI) has lost to opposition parties, although recently it won back the municipal government—with the usual allegations of electoral fraud. Worried by the earlier defeat, the PRI has tried to make the town a model of good government.

I went to Matamoros looking for the new mayor, but first I found a man reputed by U.S. police to be a mobster—by his own account, merely a restaurateur. At a fiesta by the river outside town was Juan N. Guerra, or just "Juan N." to locals who seem to cringe at the name. Not long before, the town's other alleged gang boss, Casimiro (El Cacho) Espinosa, was wounded by a would-be assassin and hospitalized. Then a dozen or so gunmen pulled up in front of the hospital in an armored car and with automatic rifles and grenades tore through the hospital, killing seven, including El Cacho and his sister. Juan N. was blasé about the incident. "El Cacho earned fame by dying," the silver-haired old man said smoothly as a gaggle of his *pistoleros* crowded around. "He talked a lot but he paid with his life."

Juan N.'s nephew Jesús Roberto Guerra—the mayor of Matamoros—was at the fiesta. The mayor explained how the PRI had been stung by its earlier electoral defeat in his town and had decided to pick a dark-horse reformer like himself. "It was difficult for the party to choose me," he said, "but they needed somebody who didn't have to steal. I'm already rich."

Could the opposition do any better? The National Action Party (PAN) has made its reputation campaigning against corruption in government. PAN's Rubén Rubiano in Matamoros says corruption in Mexico will end the day voters turn PRI out and put PAN in. But Rubiano was seriously embarrassed by his opponents, who point out that he is ineligible for office because he actually lives in Brownsville, Texas. He is hard put to deny what everyone in town knows to be true. "This is like having a drunk calling someone else a drunk," he says. "Many PRI officials have property in the United States."

Despite predictions that the PRI might for the first time lose the governorships of Sonora and Nuevo León states, they claimed landslide victories last month. Their PAN opponents said the size of the vote margins could only have come through fraud. One PRI official announced his party's victory before the polls even closed. "The PRI is afraid that if they allow any opposition victory, the whole edifice will crack," said PAN official Norberto Corella in Hermosillo, capital of Sonora state.

A controversial CIA study called Mexico the leading long-term, foreign-policy concern of the United States because of the likelihood of widespread social turmoil. President de la Madrid bristles at such suggestions. "Mexico's stability has been proven for many years—for more than six decades," he said. Even its current "profound economic crisis" is actually proof that the country "has been able to react to its problems and . . . overcome its difficulties."

Those difficulties are indeed profound. The National Nutrition Institute says at least 40 percent of Mexicans are malnourished and 100,000 of the 2 million children born every year die from diseases associated with hunger. One million will have physical and mental defects from poor diet. Not long ago, Mexico actually exported food. Now it is no longer able even to produce enough corn and beans for its own needs. Part of the problem is a galloping population growth rate of 2.3 percent a year, which means that in 30 years the population will double. "That means in another 30 years we will have to create another Mexico," says Adrial Ayuz of MexFam, a family-planning group. Already the country needs another 1 million jobs for people who are coming of age every year.

It doesn't have them, and as a result, a thousand people, mostly poor peasants, arrive in Mexico City each day. The city now contains nearly a quarter of all Mexicans, and its 17 million population is growing so fast that soon it will surpass Tokyo as the world's largest city. Former president López Portillo called his capital "the most absurd thing that ever happened." The current police chief, General Mota, refers to it as a "decomposing society."

Such enormous problems leave many outsiders less sanguine about Mexico's stability than its leaders. "I don't think it'll happen right away," said one Western ambassador, "but one of these days . . . the bubble's going to burst and I can't help thinking that in 15 or 20 years there could be [a revolution]."

The question of whether another revolution is possible in Mexico drew me to the town of Cuautla in Morelos state. It's a vintage Mexican place: streets that run like a dusty argument between facing white masonry walls guarding houses with hidden gardens. This was a stronghold of Emiliano Zapata, the peasant leader and land-reform advocate of the Mexican revolution. Zapata's ideals are kept alive by a group of elderly followers who meet once in a while at a hall here, wearing ragged baggy pants, wide sombreros and long mustaches. Only youth, and crossed gun belts, seem to be missing.

Fortino Cárdenas Romero, 84, fought as a second captain with Zapata. He was a landless peasant then; now he is a landed peasant, but just as poor. "The revolution was converted into a revolution for the rich and not for the poor," he said. Will there be another revolution in Mexico? "Many young people ask me that," said Cárdenas. "I say, we would need another Zapata, but there are no leaders like this in Mexico today. They are all out for themselves."

The border with the United States is one of the main social and economic outlets open to Mexico. Last year U.S. immigration officers expelled 1.2 million Mexicans. Hundreds of thousands of others migrate back and forth across the border for seasonal work without being caught. "The border certainly is a safety valve," said Ambassador Gavin. "A lot of the best labor goes up there, the hard drivers, who really want to work." And, he conceded, the ones who without the border option would be most likely to stir up trouble at home. Legally or illegally some 10 million Mexicans now live north of the border.

It is evening near Tijuana's Colonia Libertad neighborhood, the single biggest crossing point for illegal immigrants to the United States. Labyrinthine paths crisscross the hills and gullies, and U.S. helicopters patrol in plain view. This evening there are a thousand men about to sneak across the border, just in this one place. Typically, half will make it. Many make this trip reluctantly. But Angel, a peasant who was expelled the day before after three years in the States, is determined to go back north. "There are no frontiers for hunger," he tells me. "You have the right to look for opportunity wherever you can."

II. URBAN MIGRATION:
THE DILEMMA OF MEXICO CITY

EDITOR'S INTRODUCTION

The downturn of Mexico's economy has added to the problems of population explosion and of migration from rural areas to urban centers. Poverty and high unemployment have driven unskilled peasants to Mexico City, although the country's capital is vastly overcrowded and what awaits many of the migrants is urban poverty. Mexico City has grown faster, and with less coordinated planning, than any other city in the world. After World War II, its population stood at two million; by 1960 it had climbed to five million; and by 1970, nine million. Today its population exceeds seventeen million, making it the world's second largest city, after Tokyo. Although a city of affluence, culture, and sophistication for some, it is beset by major problems—including pollution, and inadequate housing, electricity, water, and sewage disposal. These conditions will certainly grow worse in the next decade as the city becomes the world's largest urban population mass.

This section begins with an article by Otto Friedrich, from *Time*, giving an overview of Mexico City and its appalling problems of pollution, poverty, and urban mismanagement. Jobless peasants, he points out, stream in from the countryside at the rate of 1,000 a day, with no end to this trend in sight. These problems were exacerbated by the effects of the Mexico City earthquakes of September 1985, as Harry Anderson explains in an article from *Newsweek*. George Russell, writing in *Time*, also discusses the earthquake disaster that claimed nearly 5,000 lives and left some 30,000 others homeless. He raises the question whether Mexico, forced to rebuild in the wake of this disaster, can bring about the greater decentralization of its urban population that is so desperately needed.

A PROUD CAPITAL'S DISTRESS[1]

When the ragged and exhausted conquistadors first beheld the lake-encircled capital of the Aztecs one November morning in 1519, they were stunned by its grandeur. A shining metropolis of some 300,000 people, far larger than any city in Europe, Tenochtitlán displayed immense stone temples to the gods of rain and war and an even more immense royal palace, where Aztec nobles stood guard in jaguar-head helmets and brightly feathered robes. In the nearby marketplace, vendors offered an abundance of jungle fruits and rare herbs and skillfully wrought creations of silver and gold. "The magnificence, the strange and marvelous things of this great city are so remarkable as not to be believed," Hernando Cortés wrote back to the imperial court of Charles V. "We were seeing things," Bernal Díaz del Castillo recalled in his memoir of the Spanish invasion, "that had never been heard of or seen before, nor even dreamed about."

A newcomer today is more apt to arrive by air, and before he even glimpses the dried-up bed of Lake Texcoco, now edged with miles of slum hovels, the first thing he sees is an almost perpetual blanket of smog that shrouds the entire city. It is an ugly grayish brown. There is something strangely sinister about it—a cloud of poison. The pilot orders the seat belts tightened and announces an imminent descent into the murk and filth.

This is Mexico City, grand, proud, beautiful Mexico City, which already boasted a Spanish cathedral and a university when Washington and Boston were still woodlands. Within the past year or so this ancient metropolis has grown to about 17 million people, and it is in the process of surpassing Tokyo as the largest city of the world.[*] But that growth, which might once have been a point of pride, is a curse. It consists in large part of jobless peasants streaming in from the countryside at a rate of about 1,000 a

[1]Excerpt of an article by Otto Friedrich, *Time* staffwriter. Reprinted by permission from *Time*, 124:26–29. Ag. 6, '84. Copyright © 1984 by *Time*.
[*]According to the U.N., greater Mexico City, which sprawls over about 890 sq. mi., will stand first in 1985 with 18.1 million, followed by the Tokyo-Yokohama complex, 17.2 million; São Paulo, 15.9 million; New York and northeastern New Jersey, 15.3 million.

day. Novelist Carlos Fuentes has called Mexico City the capital of underdevelopment; it has also become a capital of pollution and a capital of slums.

This is the city builder's dream turned nightmare. It is the supercity, the megalopolis, infected by a kind of social cancer that is metastasizing out of control. Its afflictions—a mixture of overcrowding, poverty, pollution and corruption—are a warning to all the other great cities, particularly those in the Third World, but to New York or Los Angeles as well, that what is happening in Mexico City threatens them too.

The statistics of Mexico City's continuing self-destruction are appalling:

• More than 2 million of the city's people have no running water in their homes. Mayor Ramón Aguirre of the governing Institutional Revolutionary Party insists that 95% of the inhabitants have access to water, but for many that means one faucet shared by an entire block.

• More than 3 million residents have no sewage facilities. So tons of waste are left in gutters or vacant lots to become part of the city's water and part of its dust. "If fecal matter were fluorescent," one Mexico City newspaper has said, "the city wouldn't need lights."

• Mexico City produces about 14,000 tons of garbage every day but processes only 8,000. Of the rest, about half gets dumped in landfill, and half is left to rot in the open. One result: legions of rats.

• Three million cars and 7,000 diesel buses, many of them old and out of repair, spew contamination into the air. So do the approximately 13,000 nearby factories that represent more than 50% of all Mexican industry. The daily total of chemical air pollution amounts to 11,000 tons. Just breathing is estimated to be the equivalent of smoking two packs of cigarettes a day.

• The combination of chemical and biological poisons kills 30,000 children every year through respiratory and gastrointestinal diseases. Overall, pollution may account for the deaths of nearly 100,000 people a year.

These are figures that inspire prophecies of disaster. Says one leading environmentalist: "The question is not whether we will be able to live a pleasant life a few years from now. The question

is whether we will be able to survive." Says another, Gabriel Qua-
dri: "If nothing is done to cleanse our home, this desert of steel and
concrete will be our tomb."

The prospect of urban apocalypse threatens not only the Mexican megacity but also the U.S. The undefended 2,000-mile frontier between Mexico and the U.S. is the only place in the world
where a wealthy industrial nation borders on a poor and overcrowded one. The official total of legal Mexican aliens in the U.S.
stood at 596,000 as of 1981. Estimates for illegal immigrants vary
from 3 million to 6 million. "Traditionally," says one U.S. expert,
"about two-thirds of the Mexican peasants who can't survive on
the land go to Mexico's cities and one-third somehow make their
way into Texas or California. If those proportions were ever re-
versed, we'd be in terrible trouble."

Yet Mexico City is not some vast urban junk pile. It is one of
the most handsome and stylish cities in the Americas, and one of
the most sophisticated. It is a city of broad boulevards and gleaming office buildings, of sparkling fountains and scarlet flower beds,
of noble baroque churches that welcome every morning with a res-
onant litany of bells and chimes. In any given week there are a
dozen or more plays being performed, plus the celebrated Ballet
Folklórico, a French or Japanese film festival, a first-rate bull-
fight. Eleven major daily newspapers and six TV channels compete for the eye and the mind. The shops in the Zona Rosa near
the Paseo de la Reforma are as glittering as those in Paris or New
York City. A suede jacket at Aries or a silver serving spoon from
Taxco may cost $200. In the garden at Bellinghausen's, visitors
savor a splendid *cabrito*, roasted baby goat wrapped in tortillas
with a spicy sauce.

That is the Mexico City of the rich, of course, and of the tourists. But as in any city, there are layers and layers of butchers and
bakers and candlestick makers, housewives, secretaries, cops and
robbers. To them, the basic fact of life is that inflation, which
neared an annual rate of 100% in 1982, still gallops along at more
than 60%. The peso, which was worth 25 to the dollar in early
1982, has sunk to 194 to the dollar. That makes Mexico's imported goods extremely expensive—or nonexistent. Pablo Fernández
and his wife Pía, both 29, do not live at all badly on a combined

income of $800 a month, but the budget pinch keeps getting worse. "Forget about buying books, or getting clothes, or going somewhere for the weekend," says Fernández, a professor of social psychology. "We're living by the day," says his wife, who has an administrative job. "The refrigerator seems half empty most of the time."

Still, those who have jobs may consider themselves among the lucky. Officially 12% of the city's inhabitants are unemployed, but underemployment runs to nearly 40%. As one U.S. expert puts it, "if a 35-year-old man with a wife and children spends his days hoping to shine shoes, is he employed?" To some, the answer lies in burglary and theft, which has risen 35% in the past year.

Below all the other layers of workers come the *pepenadores*, the rubbish pickers, who swarm like rats through the reeking mountains of garbage in the main city dump, the Santa Fe. There are about 2,500 regulars there, roughly one for each ton of trash dumped daily. By picking through the pile for resalable bits of metal or plastic, they hope to earn enough to survive. Says Pablo Téllez Falcón, 45, the chief of the dump: "They regard us as the shabby people who work in the slime with a bottle of tequila in the back pocket."

Below even the garbage pickers, perhaps, are those who can do nothing but beg. On the Zócalo, the vast central square where the monumental cathedral shoulders the equally monumental presidential palace, a balding man in a frayed black suit plays mournfully on his violin while a haggard woman with a baby in her arms stands next to him and holds out an empty tin can. A block away, at the corner of Avenida Madero, a white-stubbled man with no legs holds up a few packs of Chiclets for sale. Just beyond him in the dusk sits one of those silent Indians who are known as "Marías," this one a grimy-faced girl of perhaps 15, in a ragged shawl and pigtails, with her baby wheezing in its sleep on the sidewalk beside her. She holds out a thin brown palm, but nobody stops.

The various symptoms of Mexico City's illness all work on and worsen one another. But the one problem that underlies all the others is the extraordinary growth in population. The Aztec capital known as Tenochtitlán, with its lakes and flower gardens (and an efficient sewage system), was depopulated by a smallpox epidemic in 1520, which killed more than 80% of all the Indians who survived the Spanish invasion. Mexico City did not reach the 2 million mark until after World War II. But then a systematic national policy of urban industrialization helped send the figures soaring: to 5 million in 1960, 9 million in 1970. About half this growth came from a high yearly birth rate (31 per 1,000), the other half from the continuous migration of peasants, who regard all the hardships of the overcrowded capital as an improvement on the hopeless poverty of their country villages. At current rates of growth, the U.N. estimates that Mexico City will house 26 million people by the year 2000. Mexico City's own, gloomier estimate projects an almost unimaginable 36 million at the end of the century—just 16 more years.

There must be some natural limit to the number of people who can crowd into a restricted urban area, but it is hard to tell just what that limit is. Sprawling Mexico City is by no means the world's most densely populated place, yet the demand for space inexorably devours the city's natural resources. In the past quarter-century, Mexico City has lost nearly 75% of its woodland, which reduces the water supply even as more water is needed. The city now pumps 1 billion gal. per day from natural wells (and loses 20% through leaking pipes), but that supply is so inadequate that an elaborate system of canals and pipelines is being built. These will theoretically bring in an extra 200 million gal. per day by the end of the century—when the need will have grown still greater, to an extra 700 million gal. per day.

The pumping of so much water out of the subsoil has caused parts of the city to sink, in some places as much as 30 ft., a process worsened by periodic earthquakes. The redoubtable Palace of Fine Arts, which looks rather like some turn-of-the-century world's fair pavilion made of vanilla ice cream, has sunk nearly 10 ft. since it was completed in 1934. The 16th century church of San Francisco, which has sunk 5 ft., can be approached only by going down a flight of stone stairs. At the shrine of Our Lady of Guadalupe, just north of the city, the original basilica tilts forward and sideways at such an alarming angle that it has had to be closed.

Mexico City has another natural peculiarity that makes it unable to support its millions. At 7,350 ft., it is one of the highest cities in the world, and yet it lies in a 50-mile-wide basin surrounded by mountains rising 3,000 ft. higher, notably the snow-covered volcanoes Popocatépetl and Iztaccíhuatl. ("The two monsters," D.H. Lawrence wrote of them, "watching gigantically and terribly over their lofty, bloody cradle of men . . . murmuring like two watchful lions.") The thin air not only contains 30% less oxygen than at sea level but makes auto engines produce nearly twice as much carbon monoxide and hydrocarbon pollution. Then, when the city's befouled air rises, the mountains trap it in the virtually permanent smog that now blocks the snowy crests from sight. The 14 million new saplings that the city planted on many streets between 1976 and 1982 are already withering and turning yellow. Every once in a while an enterprising reporter tests the air by putting a caged bird in the middle of the Zócalo; the bird customarily collapses and dies within two hours.

Technology, according to the dreams of urban planners, is supposed to solve such problems, but in a swollen megalopolis like Mexico City, solutions keep lagging behind the growing needs. Consider, for example, the question of how to get increasing millions of people to their jobs. Seventeen years ago, the government girded Mexico City with the six-lane Periferico, which is now one long series of traffic jams (on a reasonably typical afternoon, a one-mile stretch contained twelve broken-down cars).

Since more highways attract more cars, the newer urban theories insist on mass transit. Mexico City's 69-mile French-built subway system, started in 1969 and still expanding, is a marvel: clean, fast, comfortable and almost free (a ride costs less than 1¢). But it carries 4 million riders a day, and at rush hours the crush is so intense that the authorities gallantly (or chauvinistically) reserve certain cars for women only.

Technology is supposed to guard people's health against a polluted environment, and, according to government statistics, it is doing exactly that. One major reason for the population increase is that Mexico City's death rate declined from 9.6 to 6.7 per 1,000 during the 1970s. The health ministry operates not only six large hospitals but 217 local health centers, and there are hundreds of private hospitals and clinics. However, some experts doubt the rosy figures. "We calculate that 50% of the Mexico City population has no access to medical treatment," says Luís Sánchez Aguilar, head of the opposition Social Democrats.

David Benítez Mendoza, 29, is one of nine doctors working at a new public clinic in Chimalhuacán, typical of the shantytown suburbs that ring Mexico City. Most of its 120,000 residents live in shacks of concrete and corrugated steel. The streets are unpaved, and there is virtually no sewage system. "People are eating excrement every day without being aware of it," say Benítez. He estimates that the number infested with parasites is close to 100%. Chronic anemia is common along with malnutrition and respiratory illness, even tuberculosis. "We're fighting," he says, but his clinic has no beds, no ambulances, little equipment. . . .

AGAINST ALL ODDS[2]

They lined up day after day, seeking family members and friends among the disfigured and decomposing bodies that filled two tents in Mexico City's Social Security baseball stadium last week. Among the bereaved were Francisco and Pedro Ortiz García, who had worked for 72 hours to extricate the battered remains of their brother Pablo from the downtown ruins of the Commerce and Industrial Development Secretariat. While trucks, ambulances and hearses continued to deliver their grim cargoes to the makeshift morgue, the Ortiz brothers waited to formally identify the body that lay near blocks of melting ice. "We don't place blame on anybody," said Francisco. "We [only] wish to bury him as soon as possible."

Such scenes were all too common as Mexico City began digging out from the two vicious earthquakes that hit the capital two weeks ago. According to police reports, more than 4,700 people

[2]Reprint of an article by Harry Anderson, *Newsweek* staffwriter. Reprinted by permission from *Newsweek*, 106:38–40. O. 7, '85. Copyright © 1985 by *Newsweek*.

died in the catastrophe. But most private observers regarded that
figure as far too low. As bone-weary rescue workers continued to
comb through the wreckage, victims were beginning to be identified more by the smell of decomposition than by hard digging.

With many bodies buried for nine full days, the government
halted almost all of its official searches for survivors by the weekend. But for most of the week, displays of courage were common
occurrences as Mexican and foreign crews crawled into dark
crevices or dug among the rubble of structurally weakened buildings in the increasingly forlorn hope of finding living victims.
Equipped with special ultrasound detectors, a large team of
Frenchmen managed to rescue 35 survivors, winning instant national acclaim. At the Nuevo León condominiums, operatic tenor
Plácido Domingo busily operated a command post. The bodies of
four of his relatives were finally recovered from the rubble.
"Plácido Domingo has won the heart of all Mexicans," declared
Mexico's leading philosopher, Octavio Paz. "His is a typical case
of what has happened. In every sector a leader has emerged."

Newborn Infants: And amid the carnage there were small
miracles. Rescue crews managed to pull at least eight newborn infants from the ruins of two hospitals. The extra fluid in their tiny
bodies apparently helped to keep them alive, and their chances of
survival appeared astonishingly good. "They're durable, made in
Mexico," exclaimed Lt. Col. Rolando Cuevas Uribe, chief of pedi-
atrics at the still-standing Military Hospital.

As the magnitude of the tragedy became apparent, Mexico
was flooded with offers of foreign aid. Arriving at the scene of the
disaster, Nancy Reagan personally presented a U.S. Treasury
check for $1 million as a small down payment toward a rebuilding
effort expected to cost a minimum of $2 billion. The World Bank
and Inter-American Development Bank pledged to divert a total
of $1.1 billion in existing Mexican loan programs to reconstruc-
tion aid. Perhaps predictably, the generosity was tempered in
some instances by the suspicion that money donated to the government's official Fondo de Reconstrucción might be raked off
through corruption. "We would rather make a direct contribution
than go through the bureaucracy," says Lorenzo Meyer, a historian and political scientist at the Colegido de Mexico. "This is a

demonstration of lack of confidence, and I hope the government absorbs it positively."

There is little doubt that the reconstruction effort will be immense. Some 400 buildings crumbled in the twin quakes; another 700 were severely damaged. The tremors destroyed two of the city's largest hospitals and numerous government and private office buildings and damaged or leveled more than 200 schools. According to official figures, 31,000 *capitalinos* were suddenly homeless; foreign diplomats and international relief officials placed the real figure as high as a quarter of a million. Many will not find new shelter soon. Government employees are likely to be eligible for federal loans, but banks have not given out money for private housing in months. And when they have, the terms have been generally prohibitive—a 50 percent down payment entitling a home buyer to a five-year mortgage at 60 percent interest.

Optimists noted that Mexico's industrial plant remained intact, its vital oilfields undamaged. Subways, railroads, highways and ports continued to operate normally, and aside from computers and switchboards, little needed to be imported. Reconstruction costs of about $2 billion are not beyond the means of a nation whose economic output is an estimated $188 billion a year.

The fact is, however, that Mexico has seldom lived within its means. Its foreign debt stands at $97 billion, the second highest in the developing world, and even before the earthquake the government had been seeking an additional $2 billion to $3 billion in international loans. Yet with oil prices continuing to fall, Mexico was earning barely enough to finance vital imports and pay the $11 billion in annual interest on its existing debts. Following the earthquakes, the country's already-ailing tourism industry was also certain to slip some more.

Financial Tremors: However unwillingly, Mexico will have to depend on outside aid. Last week Finance Minister Jesús Silva Herzog met in Washington with U.S. Treasury Secretary James Baker. While officials refused to disclose any details of the meeting, a prime topic was undoubtedly Mexico's relations with the International Monetary Fund. Just hours before the first tremors hit the capital, the IMF announced that Mexico had failed to meet its financial targets and was thus ineligible for a $900 million loan. In the wake of the disaster, that posture will probably change, but U.S. officials worried that Mexico might use the reconstruction effort as an excuse for failing to address the underlying problems of the economy. One influential Mexican economist suggested that the country now has an opportunity to restructure its debt on terms that are less austere. But private bankers, who will have to provide Mexico with the bulk of its new loans, will be reluctant to go along. "Don't come to me with humanitarian bullshit," exclaimed a prominent U.S. banker in Mexico City. "If you have humanitarian bullshit, go to the World Bank."

Although Mexico will receive large amounts of international aid, it will have to bear most of the reconstruction costs itself. That presents both a problem and an opportunity. The prospect of yet a fourth year of austerity is sure to create more anxiety, and thousands of homeless Mexicans marched down Mexico City's Paseo de la Reforma on Friday to demand emergency housing aid. But President Miguel de la Madrid Hurtado has the opportunity to enlist the Mexican people in the cause of a tangible goal. "People can judge the government by what they see," says political-scientist historian Meyer. "If reconstruction is accomplished in a way people think is adequate, the government can gain credibility." In particular, Mexicans are disappointed with the results of de la Madrid's much-heralded anticorruption campaign. Now, says a U.S. State Department official, the earthquake "might put some of the corruption that de la Madrid has talked against in human terms. It will give him the force to be able to say, 'Woe to him who tries to line his pockets with earthquake-relief money.'"

The rescue efforts last week did little to augment the government's credibility. Reports from the disaster sites suggested that an appalling lack of coordination—and even cooperation—was impeding the search for survivors. On Tuesday afternoon a seven-member rescue team from Dade County, Fla., abruptly left the wreckage of the huge Juárez Hospital after a Mexican engineer proposed to begin demolition work while some buried victims were still believed to be alive. The demolition was eventually postponed, and two infants were rescued from the wreckage the following day. In a press conference, the leader of a 68-member West

German contingent expressed his complaints out loud. "More people could have been saved from the rubble if there had been better coordination with troops and police," he insisted. In other instances, rescue efforts began only after a lengthy delay. "We had assumed that the Continental Hotel had been completely evacuated," said U.S. Ambassador John Gavin. "As it turned out, it hadn't. We sent teams in there [and] they did find bodies. But unfortunately no one was found alive."

National Disaster: Other questions arose about the government's estimates of the death toll. Eight days after the first quake an Interior Ministry official handed out press releases saying that only 1,840 bodies had been recovered. Earlier, police sources put the number at 4,600—and many critics regarded even that figure as preposterously low. "You can't believe half the stuff the government is saying," said a leader of the American community in Mexico City. "I spoke with the son of the former president of the Red Cross, who says they estimate the death toll at between 20,000 and 25,000." Officials bristled, however, at the suggestion that they were deliberately minimizing the extent of the tragedy. "This isn't a political crisis," snapped Under Secretary of the Interior Fernando Pérez Correa. "This is a national disaster."

By the weekend the rescue efforts were all but over. To prevent the threat of infection the government must soon begin the job of bulldozing and demolition—and in some way that task may be symbolic of larger change. With its tremendous concentration of government power and industry, Mexico City has become a magnet for rural peasants, making the world's second largest city a frightening paradigm of uncontrolled growth. Now the government has the opportunity to rebuild its centers of power elsewhere, spreading its wealth and influence to the countryside and making Mexico a more truly federal state. Such a move might not transform Mexico's institutions or economy, but at least it would be a start. Handled properly, says Paz, the rebuilding "can be the beginning of a new Mexico."

MIRACLES AMID THE RUINS[3]

Battered and dazed, Mexico City began the long struggle back from chaos last week. In the center of the world's biggest megalopolis, where the country's worst earthquake in decades had wreaked its most severe devastation, the stench of death hung over piles of rubble. Squads of masked and helmeted rescue workers scrambled desperately, looking for—and sometimes finding—sparks of life in a jumble of concrete and steel debris. There were moments of celebration as the squads retrieved a succession of newborn infants after days of burial. There were also 50 seconds of panic late in the week as a moderate aftershock caused buildings to sway but left little additional damage.

Even as emergency aid poured into the Mexican capital from the U.S. and elsewhere, the cries for help beneath the rubble grew weaker and the death toll continued to mount. So did complaints among Mexicans and some foreign relief workers that the government of President Miguel de la Madrid Hurtado had handled the crisis less than adequately.

At week's end the death toll from the Sept. 19 quake had risen to nearly 4,700, including at least five Americans. An additional 30,000 people were injured, and at least 1,500 were missing. The number of homeless in the capital hovered around 40,000. Elsewhere in the country, authorities listed about 300 people as killed or injured. Meanwhile the U.S. National Earthquake Information Service announced that the great quake registered 8.1 on the Richter scale, meaning that it has released three times as much energy as the previously announced 7.8 reading.

The full impact of the calamity was brought home at burial grounds like the dusty San Lorenzo Tezonco cemetery on the southern outskirts of Mexico City. On a typical day last week, hundreds of bereaved relatives filed through San Lorenzo to pay their last respects to loved ones buried in hastily fashioned wooden coffins. Some 170 people were interred during a single day, a total

[3]Reprint of an article by George Russell, *Time* staffwriter. Reprinted by permission from *Time*, 126:36–38. O. 7, '85. Copyright © 1985 by *Time*.

that did not include the mass burial of an unknown number of mangled, unidentified corpses.

Yet the disaster could have been far worse. In much of the 890 sq. mi. of Mexico City, an area that is home to 18 million people, life had returned to something akin to normal last week. The most severe damage was confined to a 13-sq.-mi. zone that encompasses the city's business district. Even there, the pattern of damage was quirky. Said Richard Bonneau, a member of a French rescue team that arrived in Mexico City two days after the quake: "We thought we would find one part of the city destroyed. But it's a building here and a building there."

The helter-skelter pattern of devastation left the city studded with contrasts. The capital's tallest buildings, the Pemex Tower (46 stories) and the Latin American Tower (43 stories), both designed to sway flexibly during an earthquake, were untouched. Less than two miles away, between 50 and 60 employees of the TV network Televisa died when their five-story office building collapsed. About half a mile from that calamity, the nine-story Mexican Insurance Co. building was shattered. Next door, office workers lunched calmly last week at the unmarred Great Wall Chinese restaurant.

In all, city officials now estimate that about 2,500 buildings were destroyed or badly damaged in the original quake and a heavy (7.5 on the Richter scale) second temblor 36 hours later. Many of the buildings that came crashing down were constructed of brick or concrete rather than structural steel. That led to charges by several local critics last week that corrupt building practices had been a major factor in the calamity. The government promised an investigation.

Rescue workers were less concerned with future retributions than with current relief efforts. There they had reason for both hope and frustration. After initial hesitation, the proud Mexicans, who historically have rejected foreign assistance following natural disasters, decided to welcome outside emergency aid. Within two days of the quake, U.S. Air Force C-5A Galaxy, C-141 StarLifter and C-130 Hercules transports were flying into Mexico City's Benito Juárez airport from eight U.S. air bases. Their cargo holds were filled with portable generators, jackhammers, jacks and winches. The planes also ferried in sleeping bags, cots, blankets and, ominously, 5,000 rubberized body bags. By week's end about 350 tons of U.S. supplies had been airlifted, along with some 250 rescue personnel.

Other governments pitched in as well. France sent 280 rescue specialists, including 60 doctors and 30 search dogs. West Germany dispatched 56 members of a disaster-relief unit, along with five paramedics and twelve search dogs, heavy salvage gear, a medical emergency center, a mobile kitchen and medical supplies. From Britain came four London firemen, who brought with them nine thermal cameras, which use infrared sensors to detect the body heat of buried survivors.

Another kind of help came from Nancy Reagan, who arrived in Mexico City with a U.S. Treasury check for $1 million as a down payment on further American relief efforts. During a four-hour, 15-minute visit to the capital, she spent 20 minutes with President de la Madrid at his official Los Pinos residence. Later Mrs. Reagan drove to the residential complex of Tlatelolco, where a 13-story apartment building had collapsed. She commiserated with Spanish Tenor Placido Domingo, who had come to Mexico City to discover the whereabouts of relatives believed to be buried in the ruins of the building.

For American, French, Italian, West German, British, Canadian and Swiss rescue workers, the challenge was grueling and at times gruesome. The din of Mexico City traffic fouled readings on some of their sensitive listening probes; thus the gear was used most effectively at night. When survivors were discovered within the rubble, rescue teams dug long tunnels, frequently by hand, to reach them.

The labor was slow, dangerous and occasionally stomach turning. At times the rescuers had to cut through human corpses to reach the living. Doctors worked for hours in narrow tunnels to amputate limbs before victims could be lifted to safety. The physicians had to operate carefully to avoid so-called crush syndrome, the slow buildup of toxins in the damaged limbs of trapped victims. Without proper treatment, like the intravenous infusion of liquids even before people were freed from the rubble, the condition could result in the death of survivors through kidney failure.

Some of the rescues fully deserved to be called miraculous. At Juárez Hospital, formerly a twelve-story facility, an estimated 800 to 1,200 patients and staff, most of them dead, were entombed within a 50-ft. honeycomb of debris. Rescuers swarmed over the wreckage. Now and then the demand came for absolute silence as the searchers listened for survivors. Nearly seven days after the quake, wavering cries were heard on what had been the fifth floor. A U.S.-American team of miners tunneled toward the sound—and eventually reached the target.

With the afternoon light fading, the first of three babies, all girls, was lowered in a wire rescue basket down a long ladder to ecstatic applause and cheers. Miners hugged one another. Some medical experts felt that the excess fat and surplus water in the tissues of the newborn had helped them to survive for such an extended period. They also assumed that the infants, having so recently emerged from the darkness of the womb, were less subject than older children or adults to the stress of being buried alive.

The experts suggested that the greatest danger to the babies during their ordeal had been cold. Mexican doctors speculated that dying adults in the wreckage near them had shielded the infants from the chill and passed on the margin of warmth necessary for survival. In any case, said Dina Villanueva García, chief of the neonatology department of Juárez Hospital, "it was extraordinary that they survived." In all, about 15 infants and 166 adults had been rescued at Juárez Hospital by week's end, and two babies had been rescued at another hospital after nearly nine days of entombment.

Other small miracles abounded. In the city's Colonia Roma district, a residential area adorned with scatterings of art nouveau and art deco architecture, Ramona Saldaña Martínez, 30, described her survival after the collapse of a six-story apartment building. She and two of her children were removed from the wreckage after 22 hours. Said Martínez: "My mother died instantly. My twelve-year-old son also died. The wall and the ceilings came down on us, but I could breathe. I stripped some wallpaper to let the air come in."

Many of the foreign rescuers had unstinting praise for their Mexican counterparts. But as the week wore on, complaints grew

among the outsiders about the disorganization and hesitancy of the
Mexican effort. Said a member of a French rescue unit known as
Les Taupes (The Moles): "It got to the point where we were practically pleading with the Mexican government to let us save
someone." Many Mexicans were equally critical. They wondered,
for example, why President de la Madrid had waited 39 hours after the earthquake before addressing the nation on television. The
government, said Adolfo Aguilar Zinser, a Mexican foreign policy
expert, "refused to recognize the dimensions of the tragedy the
first day, so many lives were lost. They went around in circles."

Among other things, the foreigners echoed complaints by some
Mexicans that almost 4,000 troops guarding the devastated areas
did little or nothing to assist in the rescue effort. Moreover, Mexican officials were allegedly more anxious to bulldoze ruined buildings than to proceed with the painstaking rescue work, apparently
out of the mistaken fear that decomposing corpses in the ruins
would cause epidemics. Carl Heinz Wolbert, a West German police detective and volunteer rescue expert, wept in frustration at
the resulting delays. Said he: "We can touch the people who are
trapped. In Mexico it is impossible to get them out. In Germany
it would be very possible." Admitted a senior Mexican official: "In
situations like this, every minute counts, and we lost many, many
minutes."

As time continued to slip away, the odds against retrieving
many more survivors lengthened. That did not stifle the efforts of
the rescuers. But as a steady stream of bodies moved toward local
cemeteries and damage estimates rose as high as $2 billion to $3
billion, Mexican officials began looking ahead to the next stages
of the relief operation, which include relocation and health services for the living and the city's eventual reconstruction. In one
sense, Mexico City had been lucky: key industrial sectors of the
city were undamaged by the quake, meaning that the impact of
the disaster on the national economy was less than some had
feared.

For years the government has talked of decentralizing Mexico
City. The rebuilding effort may offer an opportunity. Presidential
Press Spokesman Manuel Alonso Muñoz has already said that
only those government offices that can justify their need to stay in

the capital will be rebuilt there. Even so, as President de la Madrid warned his fellow citizens, the cost of recovery will be "enormous." The process will also take years.

III. PROBLEMS AT MEXICO'S BORDERS

EDITOR'S INTRODUCTION

Poverty, a high unemployment rate, and economic chaos have put a tremendous strain on Mexico's borders. At its southern border, Mexico now faces a disquieting problem as an influx of Guatemalan refugees places a further strain on Mexico's faltering economy. Some estimates suggest that there are already 100,000 refugees in camps along the Mexican border; and Mexico fears that if the U.S. moves against leftist regimes in Central America the number of refugees to Mexico may soar. Politically, the refugees present another problem; though Mexico has traditionally welcomed exiles from other Central American countries, it may now, awkwardly, have to revise that attitude for economic reasons.

At its northern, 2,000 mile border with the U.S., Mexico is confronted by other problems. The flight of illegal immigrants across the border has vexed Mexico's relations with its neighbor to the north—as has the use of the border as a conduit for drug trafficking. More generally, the poverty of the Mexican side of the border contrasts sharply with the affluence of the American, making it a line along which the Third World and the First World confront one another.

This section begins with an article by Marvin Alisky, reprinted from *Current History*, that points to some of the basic causes of migration, both urban and cross cultural. Poverty and bleak employment prospects explain why the Mexican government has not welcomed the Guatemalan exiles. Victor Perera and Julie Brill, both writing in the *Nation*, detail Mexico's minimal assistance and increasingly hostile attitude toward these Guatemalan villagers who, suspected of supporting leftist guerrillas, have been driven into exile fearing for their lives. This has become a humanitarian and economic stalemate.

The northern border is the subject of a revealing article by Mark Starr in *Newsweek*. With the collapse of Mexico's economy, he points out, Mexico's border towns are mired in poverty, with unemployment in some areas as high as fifty percent. The smuggling of illegal immigrants into the U.S. has become an industry competing with cocaine and marijuana smuggling. Finally, James Russell, writing in *The Progressive*, discusses another feature of Mexico's border towns—the concentration there of American industrial plants that employ Mexican workers at relatively low wages to assemble parts for products sold competitively in the U.S.

MIGRATION AND UNEMPLOYMENT IN MEXICO[1]

Unemployment and underemployment continue to confront Mexicans trying to earn a living. The government has promised not to ignore the plight of workers active only a few months each year or only a few hours during the work week.

In substance, that is what President Miguel de la Madrid Hurtado promised in his first annual State of the Union address (*Informe Presidencial*) on September 1, 1983. His report on achievements and failures during the past year and his programs and policies for the forthcoming year included an economic analysis.

Inaugurated for a six-year term on December 1, 1982, de la Madrid utilized both his inaugural address and his Informe Presidencial to assure Mexican workers that he is aware of population pressures on all facets of public life.

He declared that his new administration had already begun to cut deficit spending, to ameliorate Mexico's international credit standing by making interest payments on its huge foreign debt, and to maneuver the 1982 inflationary rate of 100 percent to a lower but still uncomfortable rate for 1983. In addition, de la Madrid asserted that both government and private investment priorities within the limits of the newly imposed austerity would aim

[1]Reprint of an article by Marvin Alisky, Professor of Political Science, Arizona State University. Reprinted by permission from *Current History*, 82:429-32. D. '83. Copyright © 1983 by *Current History*.

to diversify the economy and create new payrolls. Nonetheless, youngsters continue to try unsuccessfully to enter a job market that cannot absorb them all. Even the escape valve of illegal migration into the United States reduces only partially the social pressures that have been building throughout Mexico.

Census data from 1980, income tax returns to the Ministry of Finance, and other statistics indicate that unemployment in Mexico has lingered at between 26 and 28 percent for the past three years.

As for underemployment, estimates really remain guesstimates. Even scholars attuned to data sophistication estimate underemployment in Mexico from 16 to 50 percent. My own calculations yield an underemployment rate of 20 percent. Combining it with the better documented unemployment rate, we can presume that Mexico currently suffers from a combined unemployment and underemployment rate of 46 percent.

As in the United States, homemakers who earn modest amounts from odd jobs or unreported domestic service do not show up in official work force totals. In Mexico, more than in the United States, child laborers do not often appear on company records, in tax reports, or even in social worker files. If we factor in those who are paid in cash, services or goods, regardless of their age, employment data in Mexico appear even more inaccurate. Full-time employment is uncomfortably low; perhaps only 54 percent of the potential work force is so employed.

North American public policy analysts might be tempted to examine Mexican working conditions within a framework of the modernization process, for indeed the census reports that more citizens are urban than rural, and that non-agricultural types of employment have increased more rapidly than traditional agricultural pursuits. However, despite urbanization and modernization, the Mexican countryside is dotted with 10,000 villages steeped in the traditional culture of Indians and mestizos (Indian-Spanish hybrids), who are peasants (campesinos), socially and economically.

Their peasant culture has changed very little in the last few decades: Indians haul stacks of firewood taller than they are, mestizos defy icy mountain lake winds before dawn to catch fresh-water bass, pregnant women work with infants lashed to their backs with rebozos or traditional shawls. As these mothers milk their goats or beat clothes clean on river rocks even the four-color souvenir postcards cannot capture the variety of their tasks.

Data banks can computerize work force profiles, telling us much in the aggregate about where Mexico stands in terms of employment, living standards, population mobility, migration, and related political activity. But campesinos are still pulling wooden plows because of a local shortage of farm animals. In the northern Mexican borderlands nearest the United States, mechanized plows, tractors and jeeps are commonplace. But in the southern regions of Oaxaca, Chiapas, Campeche, and Tabasco, hundreds of thousands of workers wield hoes and machetes to clear patches of soil for planting.

In provincial cities, industrial plants and retail stores take advantage of computerized bank statements. But in villages and small towns, a peasant barter trade persists, a trade that was functioning before the first adding machines were imported into Mexico late in the nineteenth century.

Culturally, rural Mexico retains the fatalistic cultural patina of white cotton work clothes, thatched-roof huts, and well water fetched with buckets. Urban Mexico has accepted traffic congestion, mass transit, credit-card debt, tax obligations, and the anxiety engendered by national and world affairs. Even rural isolation has been pierced by political dialogue by the mass media. Radio can be heard everywhere and television almost everywhere.

Until a few years ago, the quantity and quality of news reports on Mexican radio did not constitute a genuine substitute for a daily newspaper, even though several million Mexicans were and are today marginally literate or semiliterate. In the early 1970's, the number of newscasts on radio throughout the day increased several-fold. In 1983, however, the cost of a big-city newspaper exceeded the cost of a loaf of bread or the tortilla equivalent. In short, radio has Mexicans by the ears and although programming depends more on music and soap operas, information programs are ever present.

Daily reiteration on radio of the material trends in the nation and the world reinforce the revolution of rising expectations that makes peasants restless and frequently propels the unemployed to migrate to the large cities of Mexico or northward into the United States in search of employment and adequate income.

Even when new factories open and even when job requirements are set low enough to include the unskilled as well as the semiskilled, those hired may not be adult males. A case in point is found in the *maquiladoras* or assembly plants that dot the entire Mexican–United States border from Tijuana, opposite San Diego, to Matamoros, south of Brownsville. In 1982, throughout the Mexican borderlands, there were 462 United States–owned assembly plants employing 105,000 full-time assembly-line workers, 70 percent of them women. A 1983 spot check at border assembly plants in Nogales, Mexicali, Tijuana, and Ciudad Juarez found that the employees were women for the most part in the 18–35 year age bracket. There were almost no heads of households.

Migration

In contrast, a vast majority of the Mexican migrants streaming into the United States seeking jobs are men. Among both legal immigrants with visas or work permits and the larger number of illegal aliens, there are some women, rarely more than 25 percent. Because these migrants are illegal or without documents, a precise summation of data is impossible. However, among women in the temporary detention center at El Centro, California (where Mexicans await deportation to Mexico), the age for women detainees consistently remains lower than the average for the men. Hospital records sometimes set the illegal aliens into better focus. For example, during August, 1980–March, 1981, 13.2 percent of all live births in Los Angeles County were to illegal Mexican immigrant mothers. Pregnant women sometimes make the journey from deep inside the republic of Mexico to the United States so that their offspring will be native-born Americans.

The popular stereotype of a Mexican migrant is a farmhand, a bracero. Certainly the United States–Mexican Bracero Treaty in force during 1942–1948 and extended after a few weeks suspension for 1948–1964, helped formulate that conception. Begun as a wartime necessity when American men were being drafted into the armed forces, the treaty allowed 800,000 Mexican farmhands a year to come into the United States to harvest crops. Pressures from Mexican-American politicians fearing foreign competition helped defeat attempts to continue the agreement in 1964; subsequent attempts to revive the treaty failed. Only if the Simpson-Mazzoli Immigration Law were enacted in 1984 would the wholesale migration of braceros recur.

In 1980, Ronald Grennes of the Border Research Institute reported to the United States Congress on his field research in urban and rural Mexico between 1973 and 1980. He summarized:

[The] new pattern of illegal migration from Mexico to the United States . . . differs dramatically in most essential aspects from the traditional pattern of short-term, circular migration from rural Mexico. Briefly, we have found that illegal urban Mexican workers are much better educated than the typical rural migrant . . . are finding decidedly non-marginal jobs in industry, construction and service areas in large northern cities, earning almost twice as much per hour as rural migrants, tending to stay in the United States three times longer . . . and expressing a much greater interest in considering permanent residency in the United States.

After studying illegal immigration from Mexico extensively, Wayne Cornelius reported in 1982 that since the late 1960's there has been a higher incidence of permanent settlement in the United States by illegal Mexican aliens and longer periods of working, the increase being gradual but steady. Those Mexican migrants who settle permanently in the United States often send for their families and therefore stop repatriating part of their earnings. Thus the rise in the number of aliens not returning home becomes a concern not only of the American government but also of the Mexican government, because Mexican citizens working in the United States formerly repatriated several millions of dollars a year in hard currency into the ailing Mexican economy.

Mexicans staying in the United States for longer periods of time become increasingly involved with welfare benefits. Those coming northward for a brief harvesting season do not remain long enough to participate in food stamps, aid for dependent children, or similar programs. In one 1982 study of illegal aliens in California, one-fifth of the Mexican women interviewed said that their families participated in Medi-Cal health services, received food stamps, and figured in compensation as computed by the federal AFDC (Aid to Families with Dependent Children).

In 1981, similar findings came from Tucson, Arizona, and San Antonio, Texas. When Mexican migrant families become aware of American welfare benefits, the few benefits available from the Mexican government seem token by comparison.

For example, Mexico has no food stamp program for unemployed and low-income workers, although its Basic Commodities Corporation (CONASUPO or Compañía Nacional de Susistencias Populares) operates thousands of retail food stores all over the republic, selling basic food at cost plus a small operating fee. CONASUPO purchases offer one-tenth of the subsidy of American food stamp purchases, not in absolute dollar value, but in percentages of minimum-wage incomes based on a 40-hour week.

The Mexican Institute of Social Security (IMSS or Instituto Mexicano de Seguro Social) hospital and clinic services serve barely one-fourth of the full-time wage earners who pay 8 percent of their salaries into the program, and do not serve the unemployed and the part-time or underemployed. Again, returning migrants who have received medical welfare benefits in the United States are shocked when they return to their home towns to find that a first aid station for desperate emergency cases is their principal health facility.

Rural to Urban Migration

Within Mexico itself, rural citizens have been streaming to the cities for the last 30 years, and in the last three or four years the largest metropolitan areas have become compacted and congested. Cardboard houses and tin shacks are not a new social phenomenon in Mexico, but the recent strain on metropolitan services has prompted ad hoc relief.

For instance, in metropolitan Tijuana, just south of the United States border, only 60 percent of the population has potable water piped into dwellings; in 1983 40 percent had to buy drinking water from trucks or other vendors. Census figures show that the state of Baja California Norte increased in population from a 1970 total of 871,000 to a 1980 total of 1,228,000, with most of that increment in or near the cities of Tijuana and Mexicali. Neither metropolitan area could cope with the influx of new residents from the hinterlands fast enough to maintain a basic service like running water, even though funding for such an operation comes not from the meager tax resources of municipalities but from the federal Junta de Agua Potable (Potable Water Board).

Almost 60 percent urban, Mexico's population presents a pattern of demographic disequilibrium. Because job opportunities, water and other basic necessities are not evenly distributed, and because only 14 percent of Mexico's territory can be cultivated for farming or ranching (including irrigated plots), Mexicans crowd into certain regions. Although four out of ten Mexicans remain rural residents, six out of ten rush to the cities. Within 50 miles (80 kilometers) of downtown Mexico City, 16 million people crowd the greater Mexico City area, extending beyond city limits and those of the surrounding Federal District (Distrito Federal or D.F.) into the adjacent state of Mexico.

More than one-fifth of the population lives in three metropolitan areas, greater Mexico City, greater Guadalajara, and greater Monterrey. In these three areas, official municipal limits have become meaningless for purposes of evaluating transportation and other basic services. Even more skewered is the access to daily newspapers. Of the total daily circulation in the republic, 60 percent of the newspapers are sold in the three largest metropolitan areas.

Labor

In the aggregate, neither men nor women in Mexico are obtaining sufficient formal training to prepare them to hold jobs in a modernizing, industrializing nation. Of the 15.5 million children enrolled in primary schools in 1980, only 43 percent graduated from the sixth grade, and an even smaller percentage entered the seventh grade of secondary and vocational schools. If President de la Madrid succeeds in getting a larger percentage of the youth into the *secundarias*, the budget of the Ministry of Public Education will have to be increased drastically. Yet throughout Mexican public life today, the official guideword is "austerity."

In order to pay the interest and part of the principal on its staggering $85-billion foreign debt, Mexico has had to cut back on welfare programs, subsidies to agriculture and industry, and to the agencies providing basic services. Thus the vocational schools so desperately needed by millions of teenagers do not have classrooms, laboratories, or teaching staffs. The austerity program has also affected wages. Minimum hourly wages in industrial plants in Mexico, which in 1982 averaged one dollar, slipped to 92 cents or 136 pesos an hour in 1983. This contrasted sharply with an average hourly wage of $4.61 in the United States in 1982 and 1983.

As for older workers, some 85 percent of industrial workers belong to labor unions, but fewer than 15 percent of rural agricultural workers are unionized. Encouraged by the dominant party, the PRI (Institutional Revolutionary party) and a succession of Presidents who wanted organized labor to have a strong voice but not to speak with one voice, Mexico retains labor pluralism.

Each year the Congress of Labor convenes. Most prominent in the gathering is the Mexican Federation of Labor (The CTM or Confederación de Trabajadores de Mexico), which should not be translated literally; it is not one group of workers but rather a federation of unions. Each union gathers individual workers together and then the union corporately joins the federation.

Other federations exist—CROC, the Revolutionary Federation of Workers and Campesinos, CROM, the Regional Federation of Mexican workers—but these lack the political power and leverage in the executive branch enjoyed by the CTM, which also dominates the labor sector of the PRI.

In the Mexican political system, there is no pretense that the Minister of Labor in the presidential Cabinet remains neutral when industrial negotiations take place. Since 1934, every Minister of Labor has publicly proclaimed his loyalty to the unions.

One notable exception occurred in 1959, when President Adolfo López Mateos, himself a former Minister of Labor, ordered Demetrio Vallejo of the Communist party of Mexico and head of the Railroad Workers Union jailed on charges of sedition under Article 145b of the federal penal code. Vallejo had ordered slowdown strikes on all railroads. Farm-to-market crops—especially lettuce, tomatoes, and other perishables—began rotting in freight cars. The President interpreted the move as an attack on the economy and well-being of the nation, and the federal Attorney General ruled that Vallejo was engaging in seditious action. Once the radical leader was imprisoned, the union elected a new leader who ended the slowdown immediately.

Agricultural workers have the National Campesino Federation (CNC), which was established in 1936 to give an organized national political voice to farmers on communal farms or *ejidos* and to those working individual plots. The emphasis, however, at first was on policy for the *ejidos* and not for individual farmhands.

From 1975 to 1982, Mexicans regarded oil as a guardian angel, believing that there was enough black gold to raise living standards and create new jobs to put the unemployed into full-time positions. Disillusionment set in when several major foreign loans came due at once in 1982. The government floundered on the brink of bankruptcy until United States and international credit sources came to the rescue. Oil profits will have to be used to liquidate debts rather than to fund industrial expansion, which would in turn create new jobs.

The de la Madrid imprint on Mexican politics is the President's refreshing frankness in admitting these facts, rather than in engaging in euphemistic deception. Perhaps the clue to the difficult times labor—organized and unorganized, urban and rural—must endure for awhile came from a remark President de la Madrid made to an interviewer for *Televisa*: "Regarding the Law of Minimum Salaries, we must temporarily concentrate on the word 'minimum.'"

PAWNS IN THE POLITICAL GAME[2]

The August 8 military coup in Guatemala, which replaced President Efraín Ríos Montt with the veteran hard-liner Gen. Os-

[2]Reprint of an article by Victor Perera, author and contributor to *The Nation* on Central America. Reprinted by permission from *The Nation*, 237:455–59. N. 12, '83. Copyright © 1983 by *The Nation*.

car Humberto Mejía Victores, has brought some superficial changes to Guatemala's foreign policy, bringing it more closely in accord with the Reagan Administration's Central American strategy. (He was the first Central American leader to support unreservedly Reagan's move into Grenada.) But the turnover has brought no relief to the hundreds of thousands of terrified Guatemalan Indians who fled their highland villages as a result of the "pacification" program that began under Ríos Montt's predecessor Romeo Lucas García, and that Ríos Montt continued. At least 100,000 of them now live under rapidly deteriorating conditions in refugee camps along the Guatemala-Mexico border.

In February 1982, when the exodus began in earnest, I went to Chiapas, Mexico, and visited the border camps of La Hamaca and La Sombra, whose occupants have since been dispersed [see Perera, "Two Cultures, Two Extinctions," *The Nation*, November 27, 1982]. I spoke with hundreds of Mam Indians from Huehuetenango province whose homes and fields had been razed in Lucas García's attempt to root out leftist guerrillas by systematically destroying their actual and potential bases of peasant support. Village elders who had tramped for miles with their families carrying scant possessions spoke in numbed voices about neighbors who were burned alive inside their huts; they gave excruciating accounts of 70-year-old grandmothers who were raped and infants who were torn from their mothers and throttled by the *kaibiles*—special military units assigned to pacify the countryside. Only a small percentage of those I interviewed admitted knowing or sympathizing with the guerrillas; the rest insisted they'd had no contact with them, and had not sought any.

This July, when I returned to Chiapas to visit refugee camps in the Lacandon forest, I again heard horror stories of large-scale massacres and village burnings, only the numbers had multiplied because the army's methods had become more efficient. Among the techniques refined by Ríos Montt is the use of "civil defense patrols" composed of peasant farmers trained to ferret out guerrilla sympathizers. The accused are beaten to death with sticks and clubs by their fellow villagers, under the cold eye of the military commander. Those who refuse to take part in the beatings are threatened with execution: their choice is between violent death and complicity in murder.

In the past two years, the official count of Guatemalan Indians in border camps inside Mexico has risen from about 10,000 to 100,000, but this does not include the tens of thousands who have poured across the border in recent weeks to work the coffee harvest. Catholic Church sources estimate that 40,000 Guatemalans have entered Mexico in the past year through the border town of Tapachula, passing themselves off as seasonal workers. At the end of the coffee harvest, great numbers of them stay on in clandestine camps or melt into towns and cities farther north. Only a fraction of these new arrivals are being reached by church relief efforts.

In retrospect, the Indians I saw in 1982 were better off than those who are refugees today. The dozen or so camps then in existence were at least accessible to outsiders, who donated food and supplies unhampered by the immigration authorities. The refugees' plight was reported in the Mexican and the U.S. media, and the response of international relief agencies, including the U.N. High Commissioner on Refugees, was heartening, although never enough to meet the growing needs. The arriving refugees were received warmly by most Mexicans of Mayan descent in Chiapas, who regard them as kin. "Today is their turn, tomorrow ours," they would say, as they shared their provisions and offered grazing lands where the Guatemalans could pitch their *champas*, plastic lean-tos, and erect mud huts. The refugees had reason to look forward to a new start in Mexico, which is universally respected for its tradition of extending asylum to political fugitives from throughout the Americas.

In recent months, however, the tacit welcome Mexico had extended to Guatemalans has given way to a policy of maintaining tight control at the border and keeping the camps isolated. The immediate reasons for this change are not hard to find: The refugees' growing numbers have strained Chiapas's economy and have stirred up old fears among landowners that Guatemalan agitators might spark peasant rebellions which could spread to Oaxaca and communities farther north. At the same time, the Guatemalan military has exacerbated the situation by staging raids against suspected guerrilla bases inside Mexico. Given the number of undocumented Mexicans who cross daily into the United States, Mexico does not care to draw attention to its own problems with Guatemalan refugees, nor to its increasingly severe solutions.

In most cases the local populations have continued to aid the newly arrived refugees; the liberal Mexican and U.S. press have reported countless instances in which Mayan farmers have employed Guatemalans as workers or tenant farmers in exchange for food and a small milpa, or patch of fertile soil. The government, however, is attempting to close its borders and to induce thousands of refugees to go home. The diminished accessibility to the camps allows immigration authorities and the government relief agency COMAR (Commission for Aid to Refugees), which have joined under a single command, to extend a *cordon sanitaire* around the camps, segregating them from the outside world. Thus far this strategy has only partially succeeded.

In mid-July, I managed to visit two of the jungle camps and I also spoke with Guatemalans who had slipped away into nearby towns. I interviewed determined Mexican and foreign relief volunteers who had infiltrated camps along the Lacantun River, where security is particularly tight. The picture that emerges from my experiences and from the interviews I conducted is appalling: aside from massacres and the systematic burning of villages, all of the conditions that forced the Indians to flee Guatemala are being reproduced in the camps along the Lacantun River, in the Montebello Lakes area and in the Marques de Comillas sector of the Lacandon forest.

The rains arrived late this spring, but with a vengeance, and have added untold hardships. In two of the large camps, known as Puerto Rico and Chajul, which are located just a few kilometers from the Guatemalan border and hold 4,000 to 5,000 refugees, malnutrition is endemic; in Chajul alone, until recently, an average of three infants died from it daily, and four or five adults every week. The heavy rains devastated mud-and-thatch dwellings, made roads impassable to relief vehicles and touched off epidemics of bronchitis, gastroenteritis and measles. Chajul is fortunate in being served by nurses belonging to The Sisters of Charity, who have been tending ailing children in the camp and flying the severe cases to San Carlos Hospital in Altamirano, which is privately funded. Children considered hopelessly ill, however, are left in the camps to die.

When I visited the hospital as a blood donor a planeload of children had just arrived from Chajul, most of them pale from anemia and suffering from a wide range of jungle diseases—malaria, typhoid, diphtheria, amebic dysentery—that were aggravated by undernourishment.

No scene I witnessed was more dramatic than the contrast between the new-arrivals ward, with its spectrally pale children with swollen bellies who stared out of large, somber eyes, and the recovery playroom, where boisterous toddlers and older children romped with nurses. Eyes and faces alight, they climbed all over me. Most of them were eager to return to their families, despite the harsh living conditions in the camps. But one vivacious boy, who had been brought to Altamirano with his skin peeling off like tree bark, had lost both parents and would be put up for adoption, I was told.

In marked contrast to the children are the old people who are on their last legs when they reach the camps and who die within a day or two, silently, unprotestingly. The community spokesman said they preferred to die with dignity on foreign soil rather than be killed in their homeland. I saw a colorfully dressed couple, who had just arrived in Chajul from Quiché, leaning on their walking sticks and looking fixedly into space, oblivious to the commotion around them. They refused to settle in and put up their *champas*. The following day they both died the Indian pilgrim's death, having called on their last resources of strength to arrive at a place in which they could shed their earthly bonds and, after a brief pause, continue the long journey toward the spirit realm of their ancestors.

In a camp of Mam Indians from Colotenango I encountered a widow of about 60. She was strapped to her loom, on which she was weaving a red and yellow striped *traje*, or native skirt. When I prepared to take a picture, she turned toward me without a word and then returned to her weaving. The look on her face haunted me for days afterward; it was as if the ordeal of her people had been etched into her features, and an unextinguishable sorrow burned in her eyes. As her village's surviving matriarch, she was anchoring its remaining hundred or so families to this patch of foreign soil, recreating their sense of community by carrying on a traditional craft, using yarn smuggled out of Guatemala.

In this particular camp, the rains had brought an epidemic of conjunctivitis among the children, but the UNICEF woman who had been supplying them with Terramycin eyedrops and other medications had not come for six weeks. "*A saber?* Who knows?" the spokesman said, with a familiar shrug of resignation, when I asked when they expected her.

Alejandro (as I shall call him), a writer and schoolmaster from a highland province, recently visited the United States in connection with the publication of a tale he had composed about a popular Mayan hero. As a poet and essayist, Alejandro is reclaiming a part of his people's heritage, not on the parchment used by his ancestors but with the Ladinos' Spanish language and a typewriter.

Before he left the United States, Alejandro's wife had written to warn him that his name had appeared on a list of "subversives" published by the Guatemalan government. She urged him to join his parents in southern Mexico. Alejandro flew to Chiapas with the last of the royalties from his book and met his parents in a small border camp inhabited by about eighty families, who had as yet received no services from the relief agencies.

"There had been as many as 200 families there," Alejandro told me when we met in San Cristóbal de las Casas, a large city in Chiapas, "but 120 went back when they couldn't get any food. I'm trying to make some money to get my wife and children out of Guatemala, and bring them here." Alejandro is living the life of a typical refugee, scrambling for food for his parents, worrying about the safety of loved ones left behind.

"In Guatemala, all avenues have been closed to us," Alejandro said. "They have taken away our rights to education, land ownership, the vote and economic betterment. I was one of the last in my village to have the opportunity to be educated outside, and to return as a schoolteacher. The only road left to us now is exile, and we must make the most of it to educate the world about the true situation in our country. We are all becoming testimony-bearers to the horrors we have lived. When my older brother was killed by the army, people thought I would lose my head and die seeking revenge. But they did not understand my resolve. I am still young. I have patience. I can wait my turn."

Before I met him, Alejandro was living in a refugee camp, where he served as schoolmaster. But after three months there, he was warned by new arrivals that his life was in danger because *kaibiles* had begun raiding nearby camps. Alejandro then moved to San Cristóbal to look for work. What Alejandro most wanted, next to provisions for his family, was the use of a typewriter. "I have stories to tell," he said. "Many stories."

One of Alejandro's stories is about the Mexican farmers who ask tired and hungry new arrivals at the camps to lend them some of their children. "Let me have your son," they will say. "I will feed him and look after him until you get back on your feet, and then you can come fetch him. I live just up the road."

Alejandro told of a refugee who had to give one of these "Samaritans" 4,000 pesos—his entire life's savings—before he could reclaim his son, only a few days after he had left him with the man.

In the forest district of San Quintín, landowners buy teenagers from refugees and keep them as indentured servants. In some cases, parents are only too happy to place their offspring in homes where they will be fed and sheltered.

The worst of these stories tell of predatory pimps from border towns like Tapachula (where the current refugee flow is the heaviest) who buy girls, aged 12 to 17, for very small sums and put them to work in the town's bordellos. Other teen-age prostitutes have been showing up in Tuxtla Gutiérrez, the capital of Chiapas, where they fetch higher prices.

Roberto, a Mexican filmmaker who has shot thousands of feet of film in more than a dozen camps along the Lacantun River, described to me the extreme deprivations suffered by those who live there. Salt and soap are luxury items, and at night the moans of starving children drown out the omnipresent jungle sounds. Roberto also said that some COMAR relief workers conspire with immigration officers to turn away outsiders and bully the Indians into submission.

"The more corruptible refugees are offered double rations, and they are given clubs and assigned to patrol the camps at night, to prevent anyone from going in or out. You can tell them at once by their well-fed looks," Roberto said. "At times I don't recognize my own country. It was as if I had wandered into a Guatemalan village under a state of siege. If an Indian speaks out or becomes a spokesman they try to isolate him from the others and brand him as a dangerous guerrilla; that is the same tactic used by the Guatemalan military. And the corrupted ones are a pale copy of the civilian defense patrols formed to encourage the Indians to kill one another off, and save the military the trouble."

Since Roberto's last visit, relief supplies have reportedly been reaching the camps on the Lacantun in greater quantities, but security remains tighter than ever.

In late July, Mercedes Ozuna, a student at the University of Chiapas who worked as a volunteer distributing supplies to the camps, was picked up in San Cristóbal by five Mexicans in civilian clothes who drove an unmarked car. She was blindfolded and taken to a cell next to that of a university professor named Gustavo Zárate, who had been tortured with electric shocks. The next day she was interrogated about the activities of CARGUA, the Committee for Aid to Guatemalan Refugees, which is the most visible private relief agency in Chiapas. It is directed by a nephew of former President Miguel Aleman of Mexico. Ozuna had only an incidental relationship with CARGUA, but the interrogators let her know they were thoroughly acquainted with its membership and activities, facts which CARGUA has made no effort to conceal. They questioned Ozuna and another student they had picked up the same day, Victor Hugo Gutierrez, about Bishop Samuel Ruiz of San Cristóbal, who heads his diocese's Christian Committee of Solidarity with the refugees.

"Where does he keep the committee's arsenal?" they asked Ozuna and Gutierrez, over and over. "Who are his guerrilla contacts?"

Ozuna and Gutierrez were released in Tuxtla two days later, with the warning, "We don't want anyone helping the refugees." Professor Zárate, who had been accused of possessing drugs and weapons, was forced to sign a confession under torture, implicating himself and Bishop Ruiz, whom he hardly knew, as fellow conspirators in subversion against the state.

These incidents caused a brief furor when they were revealed in an article in the Mexico City weekly *Proceso*, which implied that Absalon Castellon, the Governor of Chiapas and a former military man, might have ordered the arrests as part of a broad new policy of calculated repression. Whatever the reason, the arrests succeeded in temporarily chilling private and church relief efforts inside the camps.

Where is all this leading to? It may be too early to say, but the signs are increasingly ominous. Before Ríos Montt's ouster from the presidency, there were rumors that the United States, Mexico and Guatemala were planning to set up a model village program in the Guatemalan highlands, under U.N. supervision, in an attempt to induce thousands of refugees to return home. The plan was supposedly scrapped after Ríos Montt's overthrow, and replaced by a scheme under which the camps would be closed and the Guatemalans granted temporary economic-refugee status, making them available to work on plantations for a few cents a day. At the end of the harvest season their permits would expire and they could legally be deported to Guatemala.

"The camps on the border have become an embarrassment to everybody," explained Bishop Ruiz, whose kind face and soft-spoken manner belie his public reputation as a fierce defender of the dispossessed, a man who can rally 300,000 armed peasants to his support in a matter of hours. "The refugees have become counters in the power games being played out in Central America by the two superpowers. The model village idea and the dispersal plan are two of several scenarios that have been discussed by Mexico, the United States and Guatemala. One way or another, the border camps will be abolished, causing further suffering to the Indians, who, as in the past, will pay the steepest penalty for the political and social convulsions that are shaking our entire region."

In the past six weeks, special Guatemalan Army units, acting under orders from general Mejía Victores, have again begun systematic raids against villages suspected of harboring guerrillas. Fresh waves of Indian *campesinos* are fleeing their homes in embattled zones in Quinché and Huehuetenango provinces and are seeking temporary shelter in the mountains. Thousands of them are certain to make their way across the border into Mexico, where they will join relatives and neighbors in makeshift camps ridden with disease and the unrelenting misery they had hoped to leave behind.

WILL MEXICO'S 'WELCOME' LAST?[3]

On April 30 unidentified gunmen slipped into the El Chupadero refugee camp in southern Mexico, only a mile from the Guatemalan border. They opened fire, killing six and wounding six others. Two days later the Mexican government announced that it would move El Chupadero and eighty-six camps like it deeper into Mexico, though it did not say where or when.

About 46,000 refugees live in those remote camps administered by the Mexican government and funded mainly by the Office of the United Nations High Commissioner for Refugees. They represent only half the number of Guatemalans who have sought safety in Mexico since 1981, when their government began burning villages and massacring inhabitants in areas under guerrilla control, as part of a counterinsurgency drive that continues today. Although there have been occasional raids like the one at El Chupadero, the Mexican camps have provided the refugees with a relative haven from the civil war and mounting political violence in Guatemala.

The Mexican government decided to move the camps ostensibly in order to provide better security, food, medicine and services for the refugees, but implementing that decision could have other consequences as well. With the refugees out of the area, the Mexicans could tighten security along the 180-mile border that separates the two countries, thus making entry into Mexico much more difficult for the thousands of Guatemalans who will no doubt seek refuge in the months ahead. By uprooting the refugees—some of whom have lived in the camps for three years—the

[3]Reprint of an article by Julie Brill, contributor to *The Nation* on Mexico. Reprinted by permission from *The Nation*. 238:602–04. My. 19, '84. Copyright © 1984 by *The Nation*.

Mexican government could also be taking the first step in a larger plan that would lead to the return of the refugees to Guatemala. The possibility of that increases as their position in Mexico is made less stable.

Before the most recent decision the government had appeared to be leaning toward repatriation of the refugees. On January 9 it announced the formation of a special commission with Guatemala to "resolve the refugee problem." Three days later, a government spokesman said that repatriation was being studied. All the factors that point to it—legal constraints that make official recognition of the refugees difficult, factionalism within the Mexican government and the country's severe economic problems—remain as compelling as they were then.

The Guatemalan government would no doubt enthusiastically welcome the return of the refugees; the bad publicity stemming from their presence in Mexico has only added to Guatemala's pariah status in the international community. And as ever the Reagan Administration stands ready to aid its ally. In a March 9 memorandum, the State Department informed members of the Senate that if the refugees return to Guatemala, the United States is "prepared to assist in meeting their basic needs for food, shelter and medical treatment."

But the Mexican government's decision to relocate the refugees indicates that, at least for now, their imminent return to Guatemala is unlikely. While some reports, including one in *The New York Times*, interpreted the decision as a resolution of the refugee situation, at best it is a holding action. It fails to address the central dilemma that has deeply divided Mexican officials since the refugees began to arrive: Should the government officially recognize these people and try to integrate them into Mexican society, or should it send them back to Guatemala?

Officially, Mexico espouses an open-door policy under which it grants asylum to all who flee political persecution. Thousands of urban, upper- and middle-class exiles from Spain after the Civil War and from the dictatorships of Chile and Argentina took advantage of that policy. But legally almost all the Guatemalans who have fled to Mexico are considered not "political asylees" but refugees, with no permanent immigration status. They are mostly rural Indians who left the country fearing for their life after members of their family experienced the viciousness of the military government. Rarely can they prove the direct political involvement necessary for political asylee status, and Mexico, like the United States, does not officially recognize refugees. As Alfredo Witschi, the U.N. High Commissioner's program officer supervising refugee camps in the state of Chiapas, put it, "Mexico still has not ratified the U.N.'s Convention on Refugees. In Mexico, '*refugiado*' is just a Spanish word."

In May 1982, Diana Torres Arciniega, then a high-level official in the Interior Ministry, explained why Mexico does not officially recognize the Guatemalans. They come "looking for relocation and work," she said, and their presence causes "a rise in delinquency," "a rise in the demand for jobs," "displacement of Mexican nationals" and "friction and irritation among Mexicans," among other problems. Still, Mexico admits the refugees under FM-8 visas, which formerly allowed Guatemalan laborers to pick produce within fifty miles of the border for up to three months. This bureaucratic device lets them into the camps administered by the Comision Mexicana de Asistencia a los Refugiados (COMAR) but denies them legal status in the country.

The United Nations has tried to push Mexico to recognize at least some of the Guatemalans, but the numbers bespeak the Interior Ministry's response. In 1982, the U.N.'s office on refugees selected 242 of the most promising cases from the thousands brought to it each year, and Interior granted legal status to the refugees in 72 of them; in 1983, Interior approved legal status for those in 15 of the 300 cases referred to it.

Some officials at the refugee office would like to put more international pressure on Mexico to grant the refugees permanent status, but the Mexican government has indicated that such action is unwelcome. Pierre Jambor, who until recently headed the refugee office's operations in Mexico, was declared persona non grata by officials there because of his zealous advocacy of the refugees' cause. Equally important, some U.N. officials do not want to risk an international brouhaha that might cause Mexico to pull back from its vital role in the Contadora group's search for peace in Central America.

For their part, many Mexican officials, especially those in the Interior Ministry, feel that the refugee office has already interfered too much in the internal affairs of the country. Interior represents one side in the debate taking place in the Mexican government over how to respond to the refugee problem. Interior Secretary Manuel Bartlett, a close friend of President Miguel de la Madrid, and Mario Vallejo, Director of Migratory Affairs and until recently also head of COMAR, take a nationalistic view. They and other Interior officials see the refugees as an economic burden. As one Mexican relief worker says, "Bartlett would be happy to see all the refugees go home."

The other side is represented by the Ministry of Foreign Affairs, which considers Mexico's policy with an eye toward the international community's response. The ministry was particularly embarrassed, for instance, over Interior's deportation of 2,400 Guatemalan refugees in the summer of 1981. Like their Secretary, Bernardo Sepúlveda, many officials in Foreign Affairs come from academia and see the influx of refugees as a social phenomenon, a natural outgrowth of severe civil strife in Central America.

Many observers felt that the decision to move the camps indicated that Foreign Affairs was winning Mexico's intergovernmental tug of war—at least for now. But the fact that Bartlett announced the move could mean that it is part of Interior's long-term strategy. The disastrous condition of the Mexican economy is one factor that may bolster the Interior Ministry's position, creating pressure to send the refugees back to Guatemala. The devaluation of the peso, currently at the rate of thirteen centavos a day against the dollar, has caused rampant capital flight from the country; meanwhile, Mexico's economic albatross, its foreign debt, requires the government to export unfathomable sums of its precious hard currency. Prices for many basic goods in Mexico rose 100 percent or more during 1983. The situation is especially grave in the state playing reluctant host to the refugees. Chiapas has always been one of the poorest states in the country, and improvement in the near future is unlikely. According to the government, the unemployment rate in rural states like Chiapas will reach 30 percent this year.

While the 46,000 Guatemalan refugees in the camps are the most visible strain on the economy, the government also worries about the nearly 50,000 refugees in Chiapas who are outside the camp system. Eighty-five percent of them are Guatemalan; most of the remainder are from El Salvador. Unlike their compatriots in the camps, almost all those refugees—whether they have come because of political or economic reasons—must depend on private humanitarian agencies until they find work on plantations.

Guatemalans have always been in great demand on the large coffee *fincas* in southern Chiapas: the men earn between $2 and $3 for a fourteen-hour day of hard labor; women receive even less. But the refugees' relative success at inserting themselves in the local farm economy clearly piques Mexican officials in southern Chiapas. Last October local immigration officials launched a campaign to rid the area of all illegal Central Americans. They stepped up their border patrol checks of vehicles on the main roads in the area and expanded their searches on the *fincas*. The local officials consider all refugees outside the camps economic migrants who are in the country illegally. For the last five months, about sixty Central Americans have been deported every day from southern Chiapas. Lieut. Javier Salazar Salazar, whom Vallejo brought in from the army to supervise this task, described his activities to the press: "A few days ago I deported 300 prostitutes who had invaded our zone of tolerance. Our duty is to protect the jobs of Mexicans."

What happens to the refugees sent back to Guatemala? According to an official in the Guatemalan agency for migration, each deportee "is investigated by the [Guatemalan] authorities, and if he doesn't have stories that go by the books, they take formal legal steps with his entrance documents." It is difficult to take that statement at face value, given the Guatemalan government's proven record of murdering and causing the disappearance of its citizens. In 1982 Guatemala headed Amnesty International's list of human rights abusers, and Americas Watch has reported that since the coup last August which placed Gen. Oscar Mejía Victores in power, political violence has increased in the cities.

Unfortunately for the refugees, Mexico's normally liberal foreign policy has not been evident in its dealings with the Guatemalan government. In fact, some observers feel that the decision to move the camps is Mexico's attempt to clear the border of "suspected guerrillas" and thus avoid confrontations with Guatemala. Mexicans fear that the Guatemalan conflict could spread across the border and that the opposition forces in Guatemala could find a sympathetic ear among the impoverished Chiapanecos. Any official Mexican support of the opposition forces would bring certain retaliation from the Guatemalan Army. Perhaps more important, the Mexican government wants to exploit the rich natural resources along its southern border, developing oil, hydroelectric power and coffee industries, and that will require the cooperation of Guatemala. As a result, Mexico has been conspicuously silent about the military regime's brutal policies.

Guatemala and the United States maintain that the refugees are beginning to return voluntarily to Guatemala, under an amnesty program announced by Gen. Mejía Victores. The refugees dispute such statements, repeatedly asserting that they neither know nor have heard of anyone who has recently returned. One refugee said, "I understand that when they announced the amnesty some went back because of their land or property left behind. The authorities gave them some time, but later they were eliminated. I don't know anyone who would return now."

Whether the Mexican government moves the refugees to the interior of the country or whether they stay on the border, the central question is, How long will they be able to remain in Mexico at all? One close associate of several high-level officials in the Mexican government says it is "unthinkable" that the refugees would be sent back. But Beatriz Manz, an anthropologist at Radcliffe's Bunting Institute and a longtime observer of Guatemala and Mexico, fears that the economic and political pressures on the Mexican government may force it to make a "quick deal" with Guatemala. "This could amount to the return of the refugees in exchange for no more than Guatemala's agreement to talk to Contadora."

A refugee relief worker in Mexico who wants the government and the international community to press Guatemala much further said Mexico "should return no refugees until the safety and human rights of the refugees are guaranteed." But considering its human rights record, could the Guatemalan regime's guarantees be trusted?

THE BORDER: A WORLD APART[4]

The $60,000 Lalique dining table in the exclusive Jones & Jones department store in McAllen, Texas, is little more than a conversation piece, and the conversation surrounding it these days is glum. There are no more stories about Mexican men popping for $150,000 diamonds. None about Mexican ladies plunking down $85,000 in cash for jewelry. Mexicans, who once accounted for half the store's business, no longer come across the border to shop. Only "snowbirds"—winter Texans who have fled the North in their campers for some Lower Rio Grande Valley sun—wander by the Lalique. They don't buy. Just gawk.

It is still a sunny afternoon, but already some 400 indocumentados *have slipped through the loose strands of barbed wire and gathered in a series of ravines just about 75 yards from Mexico near San Ysidro, Calif. Some roast evening meals over open fires; others play an impromptu game of soccer. A U.S. Border Patrol agent surveys the scene from a distance in his pale green Dodge Ram Charger. Soon, he and other agents will set up the infrared nightscopes that silhouette the travelers in the dark. With nightfall, the aliens disperse along the many dirt footpaths that crisscross the grass-covered hill, heading for Los Angeles. The nightly game of hide-and-seek has begun.*

Deep in West Texas, at a flyspeck of a town called Candelaria, the border seems more of an afterthought. Mexicans navigate a rickety, homemade footbridge over the Rio Grande, then clamber into the United States through barbed wire aimed only at keeping livestock out of the river. There is not much to cross for here, just nine families, a two-room schoolhouse and a general store run by the Howard sisters. "It's not the end of the world," insists Frances

[4]Reprint of an article by Mark Starr, *Newsweek* staffwriter. Reprinted by permission from *Newsweek*, 101:36–40. Ap. 11, '83. Copyright © 1983 by *Newsweek*.

Howard, an irascible old-timer who moved to Candelaria from El Paso years ago. "We're part of the United States, too."

Welcome to The Border, a 1,933-mile swath across four states that is, in fact, a part of the United States, but in truth is a world apart—a third very unsovereign nation, not wholly American and not quite Mexican either, with its own customs, mores, values and even its own language, Spanglish. Family ties, religious roots and economic interdependence knit the border region in both countries together to the point that cities like Brownsville, Texas, Nogales, Ariz., and Calexico, Calif., have more in common with their sister towns in Mexico than they do with most of the United States. "It took me 25 years to find out what the border is," said Ellwyn Stoddard, a border scholar at the University of Texas at El Paso. "It's not a place where two countries come together. It's an overlap with a line drawn through the middle of it."

The border zone is one of the only places in the world where a highly developed nation comes face to face with the Third World. The result has long been an invigorating, frequently bewildering, collision of cultures. Petty smuggling, dusty sin and off-the-books immigration have always been part of the free-booting spirit of life along the border. But now hard times have created new and more serious problems. The near-collapse of the Mexican economy and the plummeting value of the peso have mired the American borderlands in their worst depression ever. Unemployment runs to 30 percent in some cities and over 50 percent in some less populated areas, and countless small businesses that once depended on peso power have gone under. The crisis to the south has also spurred an unprecedented surge of illegal immigration as hardscrabble farmers, disenchanted young people and entire families on the brink turn to the United States as their last best hope for a better life. On a single Sunday last month, the U.S. Border Patrol in one southern California sector captured a record 2,442 illegal immigrants. "The dollar has always looked big in Mexico," says John Tedford, a Border Patrol agent. "But it's looking bigger now than ever before."

'Cesspool': Those pressures are descending on a region that, for much of its length, is already the poorest in the United States.

Sociologist Stoddard calls it a "poverty cesspool" and insists "the poverty along the border, for lack of an effective and charismatic spokesman, has been one of the best-kept secrets in America." It is no secret to statisticians. Texas's Starr County is the second poorest in the nation; more than half its population exists below the poverty line ($7,400 a year for a family of four). McAllen, Laredo and Brownsville rank one-two-three as the poorest metropolitan areas. But statistics tell only part of the story. The waiting room at the Brownsville Community Health Clinic, jammed with howling children and grim-faced older people, tells the rest. "There are health problems here—malnutrition and infant mortality—that we have no business having in the United States," said John Schaaf, the clinic's executive director.

Somehow that reality, which should be a national shame, has been tempered by the region's proximity to Mexico. The border's large Hispanic population has its roots visible across the river, barbed wire or chain-link fence. Even a Brownsville or Laredo slum can look luxuriant when viewed against the backdrop of the open-air hovels without water or electricity that are home to so many Mexicans a few miles away in Matamoros or Nuevo Laredo. "We're always being told to just look across the border," says Hernán Gonzalez of Brownsville's Catholic diocese. "But the people here are poor and ought to be judged against the rest of America, not against Mexico."

As poor as the borderlands are, they are getting poorer. A year ago Brownsville's Elizabeth Street, a dingy downtown strip of Spanish-language signs and retail shops a stone's throw from the international bridge, was packed with Mexican shoppers; its sales volume per square foot rivaled Rodeo Drive's in Beverly Hills, and rents were in line with the lavish Galleria shopping complex in Houston. Today Elizabeth Street's sidewalks are virtually deserted, rents have plunged to what they were 20 years ago and local businessmen say one out of every five stores has already failed. About the most optimistic sign is the one affixed to the padlocked doors of Las Dos Americas: "Close for vacations."

John Sahadi wasn't thinking about Mexicans when he opened his gourmet food and wine shop and restaurant in McAllen. Sahadi had a missionary zeal to elevate the Pearl- and Lone

Star-beer tastes of his Texas brethren. He delivered lectures on wine at sorority houses, practically gave away Italian submarine sandwiches at 99 cents and even passed out licorice sticks for A's on report cards to lure prospective future customers into his store. But it was wealthy Mexicans who kept Sahadi's business afloat; they bought the Roederer Cristal Champagne at $120 a bottle and $70 tins of pâté de foie gras. "We sell a fine wine, Château Pétrus, $150 a bottle," he says. "The American calls his wife over and asks, 'Is this the case price?' The Mexican says, 'Give me two.'" But lately the Mexican has been saying next to nothing to Sahadi. Last December sales of *bacalao*, the dried codfish traditionally served in Mexico at Christmastime, dropped 50 percent. "If things don't improve here in a couple of months," says Sahadi, "we're leaving."

Instant Citizens: Even those businesses with deep roots in border sociology and politics have found themselves in deep trouble. Margarita García, a 47-year-old Brownsville midwife, centered her business on pregnant Mexican women who, at the first sign of labor, hastened across the bridge from Matamoros to give birth to instant U.S. citizens. Lately very few Mexican taxis have raced up to her tidy, yellow frame home. Most Mexican women can no longer afford the price of citizenship for their children—the $148 delivery fee.

Still, the border was forged out of tough country and hard times, and its natives have evolved a survivalist attitude. Quite often that translates into crime. Along almost any border the crime of choice is smuggling, and along the U.S.-Mexican border these days the contraband of choice is drugs—marijuana from Oaxaca, heroin from Culiacán and even some cocaine coming up from South America. "The people who live here aren't really dope dealers in the larger sense," says John Powell, a U.S. Drug Enforcement Administration (DEA) agent in McAllen. "They're smugglers, and if dope ceased to be profitable, they'd be smuggling something else—like parrots." Indeed, there has been lucrative smuggling action in parrots and candle wax, and customs inspectors at San Ysidro regularly confiscate everything from laetrile to lizards.

Smuggling flourishes in an atmosphere where even the most law-abiding resident is rather contemptuous of the bureaucratic maze and red tape that governs the most routine border traffic. "Smuggling was never a crime here—unless you got caught," says George Boyle, a retired geologist and unofficial historian for Texas's notorious Starr County. Federal agents contend that fully 30 percent of the county's adult population has been involved in smuggling. The trade is the county's only growth industry: overall unemployment is running at 52 percent. "People here will always do something to feed their families," says Kenneth Miley, the McAllen district DEA head. "The $500 for a couple of hours at night sure beats $10 to $15 picking cantaloupes."

'Dog Eat Dog': To Tim Morrison, smuggling beat all. He remembers one night when he made $67,000 flying two planeloads of marijuana into the States. Morrison was 1 of 12 pilots who, back between 1970 and 1973, dubbed themselves the "Columbus Air Force" as they made regular dope runs between Mexico and a mesquite-covered field in Columbus, N.M. The trips into Mexico were also lucrative; the pilots loaded up their Cessnas with every imaginable contraband—stereos, television sets, American currency, clothes and even a prize bull—that brought inflated prices south of the border. In the fall of 1973 Morrison was caught with a planeload of pot. He spent 31 months in federal prison and only a few years ago returned to Columbus. "There's a lot of money to be made on this border just scamming," says the 47-year-old ex-smuggler. "There is a border attitude and that attitude is 'dog eat dog.' My attitude has always been to do as how people here do."

The DEA is hopelessly outmanned trying to fight the dogs of this war. Miley's district has 34 agents, about 20 fewer than it had 10 years ago, to cover a territory from Brownsville 200 miles to Laredo—an area so rife with drug smuggling that some of its most lavish new homes are commonly called "dope palaces." Still, the DEA has its successes. Just five days after the McAllen office burned 16,000 pounds of pot, its drug vault already had mounds of Mexican marijuana in bales and cartons stacked ceiling high and a baby-blue suitcase stuffed with 30 pounds of cocaine. Enforcement efforts are bolstered by a civilian informants' network that alerts the feds to strange comings and goings along the border. "When we see an Anglo in this country who doesn't have any business here," said Johnnie Chambers, a schoolteacher in the backwater of Candelaria, "we know he's up to no good."

All other illicit trafficking across the border is dwarfed by the ceaseless flow of illegal aliens from Mexico into the United States. The illegals no longer pursue the proverbial streets of gold, only modest advances like paved streets, abundant water and the chance to earn more than Mexico's current daily minimum wage—just under $4. The savvy and the solvent who walk across into San Ysidro hightail it up to Chula Vista where taxis queue up to offer rides up the coast to L.A. for up to $300. Most illegals can't afford the trip—or even the modest luxury of a piggyback ride across the Rio Grande on a human "burro." They rely on luck and perseverence. "It's nothing to catch the same guy three or four times in a single day," says agent Tedford. While 100 additional agents have been rushed to southern California to help their beleaguered colleagues, frustration appears built into the system. The agents know they are confronting not just the illegal aliens but an economic network in the United States—ranchers, farmers and restaurant owners—that relies on illegal aliens to fill the dirtiest, lowest-paying jobs.

Survival for an agent along the border requires that the frustration evolve into resignation. "Look, there ain't ever going to be a Mexican who if he really wants to be here ain't going to be here," says Larry Richardson, who supervises 200 border patrol agents over 200 miles of Texas river. "People who don't more or less accept the situation as it is don't live here."

Symbiosis: The irony is that the Mexicans who cross into the United States are passing through their country's wealthiest region. The Mexican side has profited by the border symbiosis; its border cities thrive on the tourist trade searching for bargains in serapes, tequila and other Mexicana. By contrast, the Mexican youths, with their blue jeans, American T shirts and Top 40 rock 'n' roll, are often largely indistinguishable from their Hispanic counterparts in the United States. The Mexican side prospered first as a Prohibition playground for Americans, later as a free-trade zone and now as a host to *maquiladoras*. More than 600

American companies have established maquiladoras—plants that assemble parts shipped from the States and return the finished product to the American market—to take advantage of minimal duties and Mexico's abundant supply of $21-a-week workers.

The maquiladoras have transformed border cities like Tijuana from clusters of bars and brothels into flourishing centers of industry and commerce. "The tables are now turned around," said Ignacio Guardia, a businessman in Tijuana. "When we want to have a good time and see a topless stripper or if a girl wants an abortion, we go to San Diego and San Ysidro. We can't compete with American vice anymore." In Texas, where generations of Texans have regarded the Mexican side as something of a permanent bachelor party, the infamous string of "Boystowns," legalized red-light districts, have been shut down except in Nuevo Laredo. There, in dusty isolation some eight miles outside town, sex is still big business—from the bars where B-girls lead a steady parade of customers upstairs, to tiny rooms where scantily clad women, warmed by only a few burning coals, beckon obscenely.

The serape-hawker, the maquiladora worker, the Mexican teen-ager and the Boystown prostitute have always spent liberally on the American side, but most border residents believe Mexico has exported more problems than pesos. Some will argue that illegal aliens actually contribute more than they drain from the economy; they pay sales and social-security taxes and seldom benefit from federal welfare, health or retirement programs. But the flood of newcomers has had an undeniable—and devastating—impact on some schools. The Brownsville Independent School District, for example, opened this school year with 1,032 new students—only 30 of them American born. (The U.S. Supreme Court has ruled that aliens, illegal or not, have a right to attend U.S. public schools.) The influx is so great that the district's maintenance crew builds a new portable classroom every two weeks. "Once in a while we stop to build a teachers' restroom," says Raul Besteiro, the district superintendent.

Robbery: The district cannot put these new students into special classes even though many of them speak no English and some have never attended school; it is required to "mainstream" them into the same grade as the rest of their age group. "Every minute a teacher has to spend with one of those children, she robs 30 other kids," says Besteiro. "Why should our schools and our citizens pay this kind of price?" About the only problem not plaguing Besteiro is finding people to teach in or take care of those classrooms. Brownsville's economy is in such shambles that the substitute-teaching list has more than 600 candidates, and there are 1,200 applicants for custodial jobs.

Up the river from Brownsville, a gigantic dark cloud of pollution hovers over El Paso, the only city in Texas that violates the federal air standard for carbon monoxide. But environmental standards in El Paso are unenforceable, since directly across the border is Ciudad Juárez, a city twice El Paso's size, where auto and factory emissions aren't controlled. "It's like trying to regulate just one-third of Houston," explains Jesus Reynoso, supervisor of El Paso's air-pollution-control program. El Paso is budgeted as a city of 425,000, but its parks, streets and many other facilities in reality service El Paso–Ciudad Juárez, a metropolitan area of well over 1 million people. Local scholars estimate that almost 20 percent of the city's police budget is spent in connection with the border. "We're using local funds to maintain a federal institution called the border," says UTEP's Stoddard. "If they want the damned border so bad, why don't they pay for it?"

Informal Channels: Border leaders and planners say that their problems won't be solved until the federal government thinks less about policing the border and more about the people living there. They insist that the only solutions are regional ones—and that their region overlaps into Mexico. To the extent that such solutions are available through informal channels, they already exist. When a home in Palomas, Chihuahua, catches fire, the Columbus Volunteer Fire Department races across the border to the rescue.

But most of the borderlands' problems are too large and too complex to be handled on an ad hoc basis. And the border, poor and remote, has always been short on clout in the state capitals of Austin and Sacramento, let alone in distant Washington or in Mexico City, where the border is a handy escape valve for a nation in its biggest crisis in a generation. Short of solutions, the borderlands will have to rely on the human qualities—pride, perseverance, resilience—that have sustained it through its difficult history. "I learned this from my parents," says Brownsville superintendent Besteiro. "If you have a hole in your shoe, don't show it to anybody. Just keep walking."

A BORDERLINE CASE[5]

The Third World and the First World meet on Juárez Avenue, a strip of bars, restaurants, and curio shops catering to tourists who spill over the border from El Paso. For Americans who want to photograph, purchase, or eat a bit of Mexicana, Ciudad Juárez is a convenient sally. They drive in, soak up the ambience around the "mariachi plaza," and go home.

But there is a permanent American presence in Ciudad Juárez, invisible to the sightseers though manifest to the city's inhabitants. To see it, one must take a frustrating drive through streets choked by traffic, bus fumes, and food vendors. On the outskirts of the city, in the barren Chihuahua deserts, it rises like a gleaming mirage: row upon row of modern buildings and well-manicured lawns.

The buildings are *maquiladoras*, assembly plants run by foreign-based multinational corporations, most of which are headquartered in the United States. Juárez is home to about 125 foreign-owned factories that employ 45,000 people—a manufacturing nexus larger than Youngstown, Ohio, in its steel-producing heyday. Most of the *maquiladoras* operate within spanking new industrial parks, where security is tight and rent is cheap.

U.S. companies import American parts into Mexico, assemble the parts in *maquiladoras*, and export the products back to the United States. The finished goods are usually stamped, ASSEMBLED IN MEXICO OF U.S. MATERIALS. A host of U.S. corporate giants—including General Electric, Zenith, RCA, and General

[5]Reprint of an article by James W. Russell, specialist in Latin American studies at Lewis and Clark College in Portland, Oregon. Reprinted by permission from *The Progressive*, 48:34–37. Ap. '84. Copyright © 1984 by *The Progressive*.

Motors—as well as many smaller subcontractors have set up shop along the 2,000-mile Mexican frontier, dominating the economies of such cities as Juárez, Tijuana, and Mexicali.

The companies have turned the border zone into a terminal on their global production line. More than 70 per cent of *maquiladora* work involves electronics or apparel, both product lines that require intensive labor for final assembly. U.S. companies farm out, or "outsource," the fabrication work to Mexico to save on labor costs.

Maquiladora managers prefer to hire teen-aged women, believing them to be more dexterous and tractable than men. Since electronics assembly must be done in a clean, temperature-controlled environment, the new factories are air-conditioned, to protect the parts, not the workers, from sweltering desert heat that can send the mercury to 114 degrees. Garment manufacturers do not have that concern, so many of their factories are scattered about Juárez in old, uncooled buildings.

The *maquiladoras* are a tremendous boon to the corporations. Labor costs generally run 20 to 25 per cent of what they would be in the United States; the work week is 25 percent longer; the pace of work is faster, and Mexico's high unemployment rate disciplines the labor force. Richard Michel, who manages General Electric's seven *maquiladoras* in Mexico, boasts of a 2 per cent absentee rate in his factories, compared with 5 to 9 percent in the United States. Productivity, he adds, is 10 to 15 percent higher south of the Rio Grande.

Though *maquiladora* wages lag far behind those in the United States and represent a fraction of the workers' productive output, the pay is good by Mexican standards. However, border-zone wages are declining in real terms because of unfavorable exchange rates with the dollar. U.S. prices affect Mexican prices; moreover, the workers spend between a third and half of their earnings on the U.S. side.

Gustavo de la Rosa, a lawyer who specializes in *maquiladora* workers' cases, found that the government's peso devaluations have markedly reduced real pay in Juárez: In February 1981, 80 per cent of the *maquiladora* employees were taking home the equivalent of $9.19 a day; one year later, take-home pay had slipped to $8.00; by late 1983, it had shrunk to $6.80.

Maria Munoz, who began sewing for Acapulco Fashions in Juárez at age sixteen, was earning $48 for a fifty-hour week in 1981—and she had accumulated eleven years of seniority. That year, she and her co-workers planned to strike for an 18 per cent raise and a reduction in hours from fifty to forty-five. Preempting the strike, the company abruptly shut down operations. The managers of Acapulco Fashions returned to the United States carrying the workers' last paychecks and some $6,000 in credit union funds. The company never paid indemnities to the employees for closing down, as required by Mexican law.

In response, the workers seized the factory to prevent management from retrieving machinery and finished goods. Funds were raised from passing motorists and, after more than a year of occupying the plant, the workers sold the goods and machinery and divided the revenues. They recovered about half their losses. A small group continues to occupy the abandoned offices.

The story of Acapulco Fashions is unusual, not in its description of management but in its portrayal of border-zone labor relations. More revealing is the annual May Day in Juárez, when there are two parades—the government's and the Left's. Both take place on the city's main street, separated by ninety minutes.

In the first parade, most of the approximately 30,000 participants march behind banners of government-controlled unions. The signs proclaim loyalty to the ruling Partido Institucional Revolucionario (PRI). Other workers, including many from the *maquiladoras*, fall in behind company standards: Young women predominate the formations, which could be mistaken for girls' high school contingents. RCA goes so far as to dress up its workers in red-and-white cheerleader skirts, and male managers bark out marching orders through megaphones.

The second parade shatters the image of labor pliancy projected by the first. Dressed in red and black, members of the Comite de Defensa Popular (CDP) march behind portraits of Marx, Engels, Lenin, Pancho Villa, guerrilla leader Arturo Gamiz, the Haymarket martyrs, and effigies of Uncle Sam and a *charro syndicalista*, or sell-out labor leader.

Participation in the CDP-sponsored parade has steadily increased—from 2,000 three years ago to 15,000 last May—as the nation's economic crisis has intensified. The CDP, the largest left-wing organization in Juárez, is a leading political force in two dozen of the city's poor and squatter neighborhoods.

But the militance of the CDP has not moved *maquiladora* workers. A tenuous labor peace reigns within the assembly plants, though there have been isolated and sometimes violent confrontations.

The *maquiladoras* run smoothly, but not because the interests of the workers are protected. Between 1971 and 1978, the government's Board of Arbitration issued 482 judgments involving *maquiladora* employees. Only fourteen were favorable to the workers.

Mexican law requires that senior workers be assured job security, but there are many ways for multinational corporations to get around the requirement. Employers can slash hours or shut the plant down for a period, thereby forcing the employees to seek work elsewhere. Companies have also been known to swap workers, eliminating accrued seniority in the process. High turnover is seen as a key to high productivity, and workers are pressured to leave when they reach their late twenties.

The border cities were opened to *maquiladora* exploitation in 1965 with the inauguration of the Border Industrialization Program. A year earlier, the Bracero Program, which provided U.S. growers with seasonal armies of unorganized Mexicans, had been canceled. President Gustavo Diaz Ordaz was facing skyrocketing unemployment in the border region—and rising unrest.

In fact, guerrilla warfare had erupted in Chihuahua. Arturo Gamiz, a rural school teacher, had organized a base of guerrillas to combat fraudulent land reform, fight the sale of forest and mineral concessions to corporations, and defend the Tarahumara Indians. The Mexican Army engaged Gamiz and his followers in battle on September 23, 1965. Most of the guerrillas were killed, and their bodies were thrown into a common grave.

The Mexican government sensed that tensions in the border area would exacerbate as growing numbers of impoverished peasants left the land and filled the already swollen ranks of the urban unemployed. So Diaz Ordaz designated the frontier region a free-

trade zone, waived imports duties, and granted tax breaks to the
U.S.-based multinational companies.

This bonanza came at an opportune time for U.S. corporations. After a long period of unbridled expansion, they were facing
heightened competition from Japan, West Germany, and other
nations. As foreign garment and electronic manufacturers began
making inroads into the U.S. market, labor costs became a vital
factor in maintaining a competitive edge. U.S. multinational companies started shifting production to such cheap labor suppliers
as South Korea, Taiwan, Singapore, and the Mexican border
zone.

In choosing a Third World outpost, business executives consider three variables: labor costs, freedom of operations, and stability. Even before the Bracero Program ended, Mexico's border
cities suffered unemployment rates of 30 to 40 percent; wages, following the law of supply and demand, were accordingly low. The
unemployment rate in the region remains at least 40 per cent today.

The Border Industrialization Program ensured multinational
corporations absolute freedom. The Mexican government ab-
solved them of tax obligations and the U.S. Government molded
the U.S. tariff code to the companies' advantage. Two provisions
pegged customs duties on *maquiladora* products to the low wages
paid in Mexico, not to the value added to the materials in the production process.

The PRI, which exercises firm control over Mexican affairs,
has coopted most of the popular movements, including the unions,
and brutally suppressed the rest. It simply rigged the 1983 state
elections: "Privately, PRI officials admit that votes were
manipulated," *U.S. News & World Report* recently noted,
"because 'it was too dangerous to lose elections during a major economic crisis.'"

Cheap labor, freedom from regulation, and political stability
have conspired to bring U.S. multinational corporations across the
border. The total number of *maquiladoras* grew from twelve in
1965 to more than 600 by 1980.

The border zone is hardly unique. It competes with similar corporate havens in Asia and in other parts of Latin America. But the Mexican frontier has a special selling point—the "twin plant" concept. A firm can maintain its capital-intensive operations in the United States and meet its labor-intensive needs a short distance away. For example, U.S. workers can cut cloth—a task that is relatively skilled and requires major capital investment—and *maquiladora* employees can then sew it.

Runaway plants deprive U.S. workers of jobs, and the *maquiladora* competition drives down wages in the United States, particularly along the border, where there is a palpable threat that more shops will flee to Mexico.

The damage north of the border has not been offset by benefits to the south. Unemployment in Mexico's frontier area has not been reduced, and living conditions have remained, at best, unchanged. The assembly plants have become magnets for displaced peasants; local newspapers warn that 100 families a day are moving into Juárez. A marginalized, "surplus" population lives in cardboard shacks and feeds its young by begging or selling items scavenged from American parks, alleys, and dumps. Some of the poor become servants on the U.S. side; a full-time, resident maid in El Paso earns $30 to $40 a week.

The movement of women into the *maquiladoras* has strained traditional sex roles. Family strife has increased, and the idled men often turn to alcohol or crime. Many abandon their families to take jobs as undocumented workers in the United States. Spanish-language radio and television stations in El Paso and Juárez regularly broadcast appeals from wives searching for runaway husbands.

Desperation is what keeps the workers mute. Challenges to the system are few. The official unions enroll only a quarter of the work force, and seem to do little more than maintain discipline for the employers. The independent unions, which are more militant than the major labor groups, have yet to make significant inroads into the *maquiladoras*.

Opposition to the system is most visible among the squatter organizations, such as the CDP, and among the leftist electoral parties. A new and important component of the opposition is the Catholic lay communities.

As in the rest of Latin America, the currents of liberation theology flow through Juárez. When the 1979 Puebla Conference of the Latin American Church called for a Christian-based community movement to raise the social and political consciousness of the poor, a number of churches in Juárez responded.

One of them was Father Oscar Enriquez's parish in the working-class *colonia* of Alta Vista. From his church, Enriquez can see across the Rio Grande into the United States. He can also see the smoke of ASARCO's copper smelter as it poisons both sides of the border with lead and other toxic chemicals. Enriquez has become a leader of the Christian community movement, which now encompasses about seventy groups, with ten to fifteen members in each that meet weekly to discuss social and political issues. The study groups have been growing, fostering a healthy skepticism toward capital among Juárez's citizens.

But even as the skepticism builds, new *maquiladoras* rise against the desert sky—concrete reminders that for the people of the Third World, growth is not necessarily development and industrialization is not necessarily salvation. If a tag could be placed on the profits of the corporate giants who have plants along the border strip, it might read, ASSEMBLED IN THE U.S. OF MEXICAN LABOR.

BIBLIOGRAPHY

An asterisk (*) preceding a reference indicates that the article or part of it has been reprinted in this book.

BOOKS AND PAMPHLETS

Alba, Francisco. The population of Mexico: trends, issues and policies. Transaction Press. '82.

Berlow, Lawrence H. Mexico in the nineteen eighties. Library Research. '83.

Brown, Peter G. and Shue, Henry, eds. The border that joins Mexican migrants and U. S. responsibility. Rowman. '83.

Buzaglo, Jorge. Planning the Mexican economy: alternative development strategies. St. Martin's Press. '84.

Cardoso, Lawrence. Mexican emigration to the United States. University of Arizona Press. '80.

Cockcroft, James D. Outlaws in the promised land: Mexican immigrant workers and America's future. Grove. '85.

De Rouffignac, Ann E. Lucas. The contemporary peasantry in Mexico. Praeger. '85.

Grayson, George W. The politics of Mexican oil. University of Pittsburgh Press. '81.

Hellman, Judith A. Mexico in crisis. Holmes & Meier. '83.

Levy, Daniel and Szekeley, Gabriel. Mexico, paradoxes of stability and change. Westview Press. '83.

Miller, Robert Ryal. Mexico: a history. University of Oklahoma Press. '85.

Montgomery, Tommie Sue, ed. Mexico today. Institute for the Study of Human Issues. '82.

Newell, Robert and Rubio, Luis. Mexico's dilemma: the political origins of economic crisis. Westview. '85.

Philip, George, ed. Politics in Mexico. Longwood. '85.

Riding, Alan. Distant neighbors: a portrait of the Mexicans. Knopf. '85.

Vasquez, Carlos and Garcia y Griego, Manuel, eds. Mexican–U. S. relations: conflict and convergence. UCLA Latin American Center Publications. '83.

Vazquez, Josephina and Meyer, Lorenzo. The United States and Mexico. University of Chicago Press. '85.

Weintraub, Sidney and Ross, Stanley. The illegal alien from Mexico: policy choices for an intractable issue. University of Texas Press. '80.

PERIODICALS

Guatemala's border refugees. Dubose, Louis. America. 151:317–20. N. 17, '84.

Oil price slide a mixed blessing. Editorial. America. 154:110. F. 15, '86.

Why Pemex can't pay Mexico's bills. Business Week. p 58–62. F. 28, '83.

Mexico's oil reserves are not so proven after all. Business Week. p 47–48. O. 24, '83.

The inroads that the right is making in Mexico. Business Week. p 52. F. 27, '84.

Mexico tests how far the banks will go. Business Week. p 21. Ag. 6, '84.

Will Mexico make it? Business Week. p 74–76. O. 1, '84.

Why only a few companies are betting on Mexico's future. Business Week. p 78–82. O. 1, '84.

De la Madrid is losing his grip on the Mexican economy. Buchanan, Ronald. Business Week. p 35. Ag. 12, '85.

De la Madrid is dithering while Mexico's debt fuse burns. Business Week. p 50. F. 17, '86.

The Guatemalan exodus: testimony to terror. Peerman, Dean. Christian Century. 102:946–50.

Cut in oil prices hits Mexicans hard. Volman, Dennis. Christian Science Monitor. p 9. Jl. 12, '85.

Congress searches for policy to deal with illegals who head for jobs in 'El Norte.' Christian Science Monitor. p 1. S. 5, '85.

A country in trouble looks for solutions; Mexico the ultimate domino? Volman, Dennis. Christian Science Monitor. p 16. O. 29, '85.

The Yaxan story. Carrescia, Olivia L. and Dinardo, Robert. Commonweal. 110:429–31. Ag. 12, '83.

Thorn in the flesh. Rogers, Isabel. Commonweal. 111:79–81. F. 10, '84.

The biggest domino. Joseph A. Page. Commonweal. 112:318–19. My. 17, '85.

Political tensions in the Mexican party system. Sanderson, Steven E. Current History. 82:401–05. D. '83.

*Mexican foreign policy: the decline of a regional power? Bagley, Bruce Michael. Current History. 32:406–09, 437. D. '83.

*Mexico's development dilemma. Street, James H. Current History. 82:410-17, 437. D. '83.

*Oil and politics in Mexico. Grayson, George W. Current History. 82:415-20, 435. D. '83.

Mexican agricultural policy. Bailey, John J. and Roberts, Donna H. Current History. 82:420-25.

*Migration and unemployment in Mexico. Alisky, Marvin. Current History. 82:429-32. D. '83.

Mexico: challenges and responses. Levy, Daniel C. and Szekeley, Gabriel. Current History. 85:16-20, 37. Ja. '86.

President Reagan visits Mexico. Department of State Bulletin. 83:22-26. O. '83.

Population conference held in Mexico City. Department of State Bulletin. 84:80-83. D. '84.

Secretary Shultz visits Central America and Mexico. Department of State Bulletin. 84:87-90. D. '84.

U. S.-Mexican bilateral commission meets. Department of State Bulletin. 85:56-58. O. '85.

¡Caramba! Jaffe, Thomas. Forbes. 132:70-79. Ag. 15, '83.

Can Mexico pull through? Gall, Norman. Forbes. 132:70-79. Ag. 15, '83.

Hey! Argentina, Brazil, Mexico, etc. Forbes, M. S., Jr. Forbes. 133:23. My. 7, '84.

Protecting the rich. Field, Alan M. Forbes. 135:42-43. Mr. 25, '85.

After the fall. Field, Alan M. Forbes. 135:93-95. Ap. 22, '85.

*Mexico: the new challenges. Madrid, Miguel de la. Foreign Affairs. 63:62-76. Fall '84.

Don't corner Mexico. Castañeda, Jorge G. Foreign Policy. 60:75-90. Fall '85.

*Mexico at the brink. Castañeda, Jorge G. Foreign Affairs. 64:287-303. Winter '85/'86.

Mexico can't give—or take—much more. Los Angeles Times. Sect. 4, p 5. S. 15, '85.

Quake and Mexico's economic strains push peso to record low exchange rate. Los Angeles Times. Sect. 1, p 4. N. 1, '85.

Solution, not rescue, must be found for Mexico's economy. Williams, Dan. Los Angeles Times. Sect. 4, p 2. Ja. 29, '86.

The rising cost of austerity. Buchanan, Ronald. Maclean's. 98:24-25. Mr. 11, '85.

A long week of death. McDonald, Marci. Maclean's. 98:22–26. S. 30, '85.

Mexico measures its loss. Posner, Michael. Maclean's. 98:28–29. O. 7, '85.

The threat to Mexico. Glynn, Lenny. Maclean's. 99:52+. F. 10, '86.

*Pawns in the political game. Perera, Victor. Nation. 237:455–59. N. 12, '83.

*Will Mexico's 'welcome' last? Brill, Julie. Nation. 238:602–04. My. 19, '84.

Mexican tremors. Nadle, Marlene. Nation. 238:565. My. 24, '84.

A political dilemma for Mexico. Perera. Nation. 239:161+. S. 8, '84.

Rescue missions impossible. Lernoux, Penny. Nation. 239:315–17. O. 6, '84.

One-way traffic. Primack, Phil. Nation. 240:661. Je. 1, '85.

Mexico City: an alarming giant. McDowell, Bart. National Geographic. 166:138–78. Ag. '84.

U.S.-Mexican border: life on the line. Kramer, Mark. National Geographic. 167:720–49. Je. '85.

Trouble on Dog Hill. Lake, George Byram. National Review. 35:822–23. Jl. 8, '83.

What next in Mexico? Lake, George Byram. National Review. 36:26–28. Je. 29, '84.

Central America's Big Brother. Alisky, Marvin. National Review. 37:29+. Je. 28, '85.

*How 'La Crisis' is crippling Mexico. Colburn, Forrest D. New Leader. 69:5–7. Ja. 13, '86.

Fire in the pan. Orme, William. New Republic. 192:19–21. My. 6, '85.

Griefbusters. Editorial. New Republic. 193:7–8+. O. 21, '85.

It's worse than you think—banking's big crisis. Dorfman, Dan. New York. 19:19+. F. 17, '86.

Mexico threatened by oil price cuts. New York Times. p 23. S. 2, '85.

Mexico gloomier on economy now. New York Times. p 54. O. 8, '85.

Mexico at the brink. Wicker, Tom. New York Times. p 23. Ja. 24, '86.

Mexico: the reluctant domino. Willey, Fay. Newsweek. 101:24. Mr. 14, '83.

*The border: a world apart. Starr, Mark. Newsweek. 101:36–40. Ap. 11, '83.

The rhetoric and the reality. Nissen, Beth. Newsweek. 102:28–29. Ag. 15, '83.

*Mexico: where 'la mordida' is king. Norland, Rod. Newsweek. 106:44–48. Ag. 12, '85.

Disaster in Mexico. Newsweek. 106:16–22+. S. 30, '85.

*Against all odds. Anderson, Harry. Newsweek. 106:38–40. O. 7, '85.

Bordering on bankruptcy. Anderson, Harry. Newsweek. 107:37. Ja. 13, '86.

*A borderline case. Russell, James W. Progressive. 48:34–37. Ap. '84.

Rumblings on the right. Kurlansky, Mark J. Progressive. 49:24–27. Ap. '85.

Chaos on the left. Rothschild, Matthew. Progressive. 49:25. Ap. '85.

Banking on Mexico. Time. 121:46. F. 7, '83.

Sensitivity but not total harmony. Russell, George. Time. 121:35. My. 2, '83.

*Mexico tightens its belt. De Mott, John S. Time. 121:48–50. Je. 13, '83.

Speak softly or carry a big stick? Kohan, John. Time. 122:28–29. Ag. 29, '83.

Union blues. Time. 122:39. O. 10, '83.

Guatemalan exiles stir tension. Time. 123:50. Je. 18, '84.

Wounded honor. Time. 124:58. Jl. 9, '84.

*A proud capital's distress. Friedrich, Otto. Time. 124:26–35. Ag. 6, '84.

Hands across the border. Koepp, Stephen. Time. 124:36. S. 10, '84.

A noise like thunder. Magnuson, Ed. Time. 126:35–43. S. 30, '85.

*Miracles amid the ruins. Russell, George. Time. 126:36–38. O. 7, '85.

Invasion from Mexico—it just keeps growing. Chaze, William L. U. S. News & World Report. 94:37–41. Mr. 7, '83.

Mexicans take weak peso with a shrug. Foltz, Charles S. Jr. U. S. News & World Report. 95:51. Jl. 18, '83.

After Mexico's vote, more headaches for U. S. Migdail, Carl J. U. S. News & World Report. 99:37–38. Jl. 22, '85.

The desolate village they left behind. Bussey, Jane. U. S. News & World Report. 99:38–39. Ag. 19, '85.

A sick economy that drives out Mexico's poor. Alm, Richard and Migdail, Carl J. U. S. News & World Report. 99:40. Ag. 19, '85.

Mexico's days of disaster. U. S. News & World Report. 99:11–14. S. 30, '85.

In shattered Mexico, tears softened by hope. Huntley, Steve. U. S. News & World Report. 99:24–27. O. 7, '85.

Why low oil prices worry banks. Alm, Richard and Scherschel, Patricia M. U. S. News & World Report. 100:51. F. 24, '86.

Behind Mexico's financial crisis. Kane, Tim D. USAToday. 111:27–30. Ja. '83.

Focus on Mexico. Wolfe, James H. USA Today. 112:13. Jl. '83.

Painful progress: another view of Mexico. Alisky, Marvin. USA Today. 112:17. S. '83.

Mexico feeling grip of new recession. Wall Street Journal. p 23. Jl. 22, '85.

Reconstruction for Mexico hinges on bank reform. Wall Street Journal. p 25. O. 4, '85.

Mexico's crisis grows as money and the rich both seek safer places. Wall Street Journal. p 1. O. 11, '85.

Mexico signs new debt pact. Washington Post. p D1. Mr. 30, '85.

Mexican leader seen weakening politically; economic policies criticized. McCartney, Robert J. Washington Post. p A29. D. '85.

Mexico tackling economic downturn. Washington Post. p H3. Ja. 19, '86.

*The shame of Mexico. Tavares, Flavio. World Press Review. 30:26–28. Ag. '83.

Mexico's recovery progress. Hamilton, Adrian. World Press Review. 31:50. J. '84.

Overcrowded Mexico City. Pearce, Fred. World Press Review. 31:56–58. D. '84.

fers of power. We also recovered sovereignty over our oil resources, carried out an extensive land reform and furthered the
goals of free public education and progressive labor relations.
Since then, the labor movement, peasant organizations, the middle
class and the private sector have had effective institutional channels to promote their interests; their orderly participation has
helped to consolidate the political regime.

The basic institutions and rules of the political system were
established with the founding of the party of the revolution, now
the Revolutionary Institutional Party (PRI), and have been
strengthened since: a strong one-term presidency; guarantee of
democratic freedoms for all citizens; respect and loyalty of the
armed forces for the Constitution and the political system; mechanisms for reaching policy agreements by negotiation; and a permanent process of strengthening social rights through legal reforms
and increasing the social benefits to public education, health and
municipal services. . . .

During these last few years, not only Mexico's political institutions, but its social fabric as well, have had to face new challenges. The urgent task has been to meet the basic needs of a
population which has grown from 20 to 76 million in scarcely four
decades. Mexico is now the eleventh largest nation in the world.
Once an agrarian society, we now have two-thirds of our population living in urban areas. Rapid economic growth and urbanization have generated additional demands and created new
problems.

Mexico stands as one of the world's most successful cases of
economic growth. Over four decades it maintained an annual
growth rate of more than six percent. Its productive capacity is
now the ninth largest in the world, excluding the East European
socialist countries. Its natural resources are diverse and abundant;
its hydrocarbon reserves are the fourth largest in the world, and
it is one of the main producers of metallic and non-metallic miner-
als. Its agriculture is diversified and its industry bigger than that
of some developed countries, such as Sweden, Belgium, Denmark,
Norway and Spain, and developing countries such as South Korea
and India. We have built an extensive and modern transport in-

frastructure, and our tourist and commercial services can compete with the best in the world. The quality of our human resources has also been significantly improved through the creation of important research centers and extensive higher education and technical facilities. Overall, the gains made in production, employment and basic services are significant.

Improvements in health care made us one of the fastest growing populations in the world. The population of Mexico City and the metropolitan zone is equal to that of all Central America. A way had to be found to reduce this growth without infringing upon individual rights. The solution was to promote family planning, which allowed us to reduce the annual rate of growth from an average of 3.2 percent during the decade 1970–80 to 2.4 percent in 1984.

Despite the population increase in the last decade, the number of people having access to higher education and training facilities tripled and over 70 percent of all housing now has water and electricity. Illiteracy has dropped from 26 percent of the population to 17 percent. Every child is now guaranteed access to elementary school. Education is clearly the key to the major changes that have taken place in Mexico over the past 50 years.

Yet, extreme social inequalities persist and the country has had to overcome an acute economic crisis. Our economy was not structured to withstand external shocks. The heavy reliance on internal industrial growth had not been accompanied by commercial modernization and increases in agricultural productivity. Internal financing was insufficient to meet the demographic pressures as they were translated into growing social demands for public expenditure and investment. An overvalued exchange rate inhibited industrial integration and competitiveness and made capital exports and foreign purchases very profitable. High oil prices and corresponding credit availability allowed us to survive such imbalances, but when the price of oil fell, expectations were modified, our disequilibriums became apparent and a chain of reactions occurred which deepened the crisis.

During 1982 the gross domestic product fell for the first time since the Great Crash of 1929. Inflation, which was 30 percent during the first months of 1982, soared to 150 percent by year-